Why will you buy thi...

−To find the inspiration to lead a better professional and personal life.

− To help you lead others − whether you're a professional coach or football manager of a local kids team; a newly appointed manager of a supermarket; a business manager looking to reset your career or someone who just wants to be a better role model.

− To think more clearly about your job; to get more from yourself and others you work with.

− To read revealing anecdotes from inside the boss's office; the personal stories of how the top Premier League football managers in the country have laid the foundations to success.

− To learn about education and understand modern-day thinking and theories on leadership.

− To help support a good cause.

− To understand that it's not always about being at the top but staying on the right journey.

This book is dedicated to John McKiernan – The Greatest Armchair Manager there ever was (16/12/1934 - 05/10/2019)

THE FIRST 100 DAYS

LESSONS IN LEADERSHIP FROM THE FOOTBALL BOSSES

Reach Sport

www.reachsport.com

About author #1:

✖ PHIL DENTON ✖

 At 36 years of age, Phil Denton became one of the youngest headteachers in the country. Before securing his headship at St Bede's Catholic High School in Ormskirk, Denton worked in sales and marketing, created his own music promotions business and was also in charge of running the largest amateur football club in Jeddah, Saudi Arabia. Denton has been studying for a Masters in leadership in education and the development of individuals and organisations through a doctorate programme. In addition, he has read widely on the psychology of leadership and is a regular contributor to national education publications on such topics as aspirational cultures and effective leadership approaches. With family roots in Birkenhead, Merseyside, he is a fervent supporter of Tranmere Rovers. The experience of writing this book has been inspiring as he explains: 'There is no doubt that the lessons learnt and experiences of football managers have much in common with the experiences of many leaders today. The way in which readers will be able to relate to these lessons is one which is truly unique, valuable and compelling.'

About author #2:

✖ MICKY MELLON ✖

Born in 1972 in Paisley, Scotland, Micky Mellon is one of the most successful managers in the Football League. A former professional footballer with Bristol City, West Bromwich Albion, Blackpool, Tranmere Rovers, Burnley, Kidderminster Harriers, Witton Albion and Lancaster City, Mellon started his management career at Fleetwood Town, taking them from non-league obscurity to the Football League. He guided Shrewsbury Town to League One promotion in 2015 and later achieved back-to-back promotions with Tranmere Rovers in 2018 and 2019. At Prenton Park, Mellon took over a side and a club with disillusioned fans, a culture of failure and demotivated playing staff. As he did at other clubs, Mellon picked up the club by the scruff of the neck and rebuilt solid foundations for their future. In July 2020, Mellon was appointed as manager of Dundee United in the Scottish Premier League. His first 100 days in every management situation has proved successful and his methods are based upon experience, knowledge and an unmistakeable Glaswegian drive for victory. Mellon also works with the League Managers Association and delivers talks and webinars for managers and coaches across the UK.

Reach Sport

www.reachsport.com

Published in Great Britain and Ireland in 2021 by Reach Sport,
5 St Paul's Square, Liverpool, L3 9SJ.

www.reachsport.com
@Reach_Sport

Reach Sport is a part of Reach PLC.
One Canada Square, Canary Wharf, London, E15 5AP.

Cover design and inside illustrations: Adam Ward.
Copy-editing: Harri Aston.

ISBN: 9781911613978
eBook ISBN: 9781914197024

Printed and bound by CPI Group (UK) Ltd, Croydon, CR0 4YY.

CONTENTS

Forewords by Richard Bevan, CEO The League Managers
Association; Premier League manager Sam Allardyce;
Sir David Carter, former National Schools Commissioner

Contents

Forewords x 3:

'USE THIS BOOK LIKE YOUR SUPPORT NETWORK'

Richard Bevan, CEO League Managers Association:

It is a great pleasure and a privilege to be able to introduce and welcome you to Micky and Phil's book, 'The First 100 Days: Lessons In Leadership from the Football Bosses'.

Football managers today lead teams under immense scrutiny with every action and decision they take open to criticism. With pressure to win from fans and owners, constant media debate and high levels of turnover, managers are under constant and intense pressure to succeed. The statistics on average tenures of managers across the leagues clearly demonstrate that time is a scarce commodity in the profession. Making a positive impact quickly is essential.

There are a number of important factors that have always been critical for a manager to enjoy a long and rewarding career. Personal resilience to withstand pressure, coupled with the ability to make a successful start in the job are vital. How you approach the first few weeks in a new role, whether it is your first job or your eighth, sets the foundation for your future success. You must survive to succeed.

Micky and Phil's book focuses on this most important time as a leader in football or any other business – the first 100 days.

With more than 30 years in football as a player, coach and manager, Micky has gained extensive experience, witnessed enormous change and learnt many lessons. He has also built a significant network of world-class, successful managers of some of the highest-profile clubs in the world, all of whom have been prepared to share their insights with him. Their learnings, experiences and insights will help managers and coaches build the skills and resilience required to survive the early challenges they face, maximise their talent and be the best they can be.

Through a combination of Micky's experience, interviews and research, he and Phil have developed a deep under-standing of the diverse range of real life, professional challenges that managers face. This book provides practical insights into the most frequently highlighted and complex of those challenges. It provides guidance on proactive actions and strategies, and draws on the experience of some great managers, who have successfully navigated these challenges to achieve success. Alongside inspirational stories from business, education and other sectors, these transferable lessons can teach leaders across sectors.

This book covers many key topics vital for improving a team's collective performance both on and off the field; the importance of research, preparation and assessing the job to be done even before Day 1; the key role of strong organisational and time management skills needed to deal with the numerous and varied responsibilities as well the inevitable information overload; the need to clearly communicate vision, plans, hopes and expectations to your players, staff, board and media; and of course, building a team and a culture that gets the whole club aligned together, to effectively execute informed and constructive change.

This book will also help every manager and leader understand the importance of having their own vision, principles and ethos combined with the attitude to push through the inevitable tough times, learning from their mistakes and setbacks at every step, and becoming better leaders as a result.

The COVID-19 pandemic has highlighted the qualities of great leaders and managers for all of us. They do not have all the answers, but they are consistent, adaptable and balanced under pressure. They understand the importance of relationships and know that they cannot do things without the support and talent of others. They also understand the importance of establishing an environment that supports both the physical and psychological wellbeing of all members of the team.

This book is a welcome and valuable addition to the library of the LMA's Institute of Leadership and High Performance. It will become an immensely invaluable resource that will inspire coaches and managers to keep learning even when faced with the realities and challenges of professional football management's employment landscape.

I'd like to give huge congratulations to Micky, Phil and everyone who has contributed to this book, or been involved in its production in any way. It is a terrific team effort and is sure to enhance and improve the performance and success of everyone who reads it.

Sam Allardyce, Premier League football manager:
Over a 27-year managerial career, I have managed 12 different sides from Limerick to the England national team. I have always thought the first 100 days are absolutely key in creating a winning mentality and culture that can achieve what you need to for the football club. Being a part of this project and then reading the final book has only reinforced just how much football managers and leaders of today need to realise the importance of this.

The work that Micky and Phil have done has shown just how much thinking goes into making a winning start for any manager. To begin with, you need to do your homework. You need to be walking into that training ground or office knowing what position the team is in and exactly what position your employers are expecting you to get it to. You can do this by talking, listening and observing when you arrive, but anything you can find out before you walk into the building only helps you off to a good start.

In football, you need to win. This book won't guarantee that, in football or in life. No-one can do that. What the advice and experiences provide is a method that can give you the best chance of winning your matches on the pitch, in the boardroom or in the market. Micky is a master at winning on and off the field, as is every manager you will hear from in these chapters. I would encourage anyone reading this to think about how it can apply to your setting. Your first 100 days don't need to be the start of your time at a new job, they can be from tomorrow, or the day you decide to start leading like some of the best in the football business.

In my mind, you've got to love that challenge. You've got to thrive off driving onto the training ground ready to start moving your team forward. People say football management and leadership in general is a lonely place. I think it can be one of the most exciting roles when you surround yourself with a driven support network. Use this book as your support network if you like and think of these voices like your backroom team.

No football club has ever been the same as the next. No leadership role is identical to your last. What makes you successful with one team will be a disaster with the next. This book is about understanding that and taking the right steps to understand the game you're in. As Micky would say, these chapters help you to 'understand the questions the game is asking you'.

I've known Micky for a long time, as a player and a manager. I am excited for you to see just how his mind works and enjoy hearing about the minds of other top managers. I can see just how much it has brought to Phil's role in education too.

The COVID-19 pandemic has made it more important than ever that leaders from every walk of life pull together and support each other so that we all improve. The idea of being a 'team' and having a positive culture and identity has never been more important than now. Enjoy reading this book, which is for a great cause, and I hope you finish it as a leader who can then give your team the best chance of answering the questions that your game will ask of you.

Sir David Carter, former National Schools Commissioner:
For those of us who manage to combine an interest in school leadership and the world of sport, this is a brilliant addition to the library of great reading on these two topics. The book talks about the challenges of creating new cultures, new ways of working, making clear that new leaders, whether in a school or at a football club, have to communicate really well.

Both roles are potentially lonely ones, yet we see in the book the value of building networks and gathering coalitions of support around you. Leadership is fundamentally a collaborative activity but where the responsibility for results and making a difference sits firmly on the shoulder of the school leader or football manager. There are three powerful messages that we can take from this book that apply equally well to both professions.

The first is that the opening 100 days in a new role as a headteacher or football manager is an opportunity not to be wasted. The new recruit is either following on from a leader who was a champion or a leader who flirted with relegation. Being clear that there is a new approach about to be taken and building the confidence of the team in you as a leader are really well explained.

Secondly, you need a game plan! What is it that you

are bringing strategically to school improvement and the gathering of more points to move your team up the league table?

Thirdly, you need to create the sense that improvement and high performance is achievable. Having a plan cements the way you want to operate and lead but being able to translate this into a coherent strategy where every team member understands their role is key to the success of the leader in these dual contexts.

The publication of this excellent leadership book coincides with one of the greatest leadership challenges we have seen in living memory. The COVID-19 pandemic has made us challenge many of our concepts about how we lead, irrespective of the sector that we represent.

What is clear is that the next few years will require resilience, determination, compassion and strategic insight to navigate our teams to create a new concept of normality. The pragmatic advice in this book will help and support us lead through this challenging era.

This book made me think. This book made me reflect. The best books do this for us.

Introduction: When Micky met Phil

AN UNLIKELY JOURNEY OF SELF-DISCOVERY

One morning in August...

On August 4th 2018, the uncomfortable heat of a hotel room with no air-conditioning and those windows that never open quite enough awoke me from my slumber. I was in Stevenage, it was a Saturday morning and it was 6.30am. There does not sound much to be excited about in this scenario I admit, that is unless you are a football fan and it is the first game of your team's first season back in the Football League.

Having woken up early, I decided to burn off some nervous energy in the hotel gym, much to the annoyance of my sleepy wife. I entered the empty gym and began to lift, run and cycle off the tension that besets any football fan on Day 1 of the league season. It's not logical or sensical but the emotional charge you feel for your club has a vice-like grip. The gym was well equipped, small but with an open door and the dawn of a summer's day, it was refreshing and the setting for the first unexpected step on this unlikely voyage of discovery.

Introduction

As I tried to force out the anxiety on a chest press contraption, I noticed another early riser enter the room. I turned my head and saw it was Micky Mellon, the manager that had just led my beloved Tranmere Rovers from non-league back to League Two.

Micky had brought our club together and dragged us from the abyss. Around three months earlier, I had been but a face in the crowd cheering Tranmere's promotion at Wembley Stadium under his leadership. Now, on this warm August morning I entered into conversation with a leader who I admired greatly. It was not just the success of promotion that drew my admiration. What Micky had brought to our club was a renewed sense of pride, purpose and passion.

Before meeting him, I had become fascinated by the language he used in interviews, how he addressed the club's supporters and the assured way in which he had established principles of excellence within a club that had known nothing but disappointment for more than 20 years.

What makes a great leader is constantly on my mind and I have studied the theories, people and approaches widely. I have also taken part in world class leadership programmes: I was a participant on the Future Leaders programme for aspiring headteachers in 2013. The programme is run by Ambition Institute, a charity whose purpose is to improve life chances for disadvantaged young people by developing great teachers and school leaders. So it goes without saying that I was eager to speak to Micky about the impact he had on the club that I love, both as a fan and as part of a case study for outstanding leadership.

My interest in Micky's leadership was heightened by the fact that I was just about to embark on my first 100 days as a headteacher of a high school. I had been preparing for this role for my entire professional career. I wouldn't say I am the type of leader that would fill a room with charisma and authority; rather I believe my strengths are emotional intelligence and strategic thinking, underpinned by a ridiculous work ethic which I believe is fundamental to success of any kind.

As I learned from Micky, we both shared the same values of hard work and inner belief. We discussed how this was instilled in us both through our parents, who worked tirelessly to give us the opportunities which we have taken. We are, though, very different people. Micky leads with an external steel and toughness that is driven by an insatiable desire for success. His strong Glaswegian accent, confident tone and demeanour would not look out of place on a medieval battlefield. If I tried to replicate that persona I would fail miserably.

For me, this has made our collaboration fascinating and hearing from leaders with such a broad range of personalities has shown me something above everything else. You must be yourself in life and leadership. As clichéd as it may sound, being the best version of yourself is crucial to being authentic and trustworthy.

However, while being yourself you can also learn from others, like top football managers, and employ approaches that can give you the best chance of creating winning teams in whatever leadership role you undertake.

Introduction

On that first day, we did not know where things would go but we both knew we could learn a great deal from each other. Despite our fields being different – Micky's football leadership and mine educational – we saw so many common concepts that intrigued us both.

'Let's keep in touch' said Micky, 'we're going to learn a lot from each other.' And there it was. The beginning of a voyage of discovery into the world of leadership. We became an unlikely duo, looking for the truth of what it takes to be a sensational leader in any walk of life.

Why we wanted to write this book

For me and most of us, we do not have to endure the weekly trials and tribulations experienced by a football manager. Those of us who aspire to leadership positions or currently occupy them, will have good days and bad days played out in front of colleagues along with close family and friends. As a football manager, the good days can result in high acclaim and joyous appreciation. However, as quickly as the highs arrive so can they be snatched away, swiftly followed by the boos of the crowd and the glare of the chairman.

The question of who these individuals are behind the cameras will be answered in this book. We will gain an understanding of the vision they seek or sought to create at their club. Then we will examine the methods they employed to embed this through the complex beast that is a professional football club. The ups, the downs, the pressure, the joy, the fame, the despair and the outcome of it all, explained to you by the managers who we think we know.

The managers you will hear from will give you a unique insight into the development of culture, the creation of a team ethic and the development of winning mindsets. We will talk in-depth about how you can apply these winning tactics on the sports field, in the office space, in a school or even leading your families through the supermarket aisles.

While we wrote this book, Micky and I reflected on what the factors are to successful starts to managerial reigns. Then, unbeknown to anyone, I ran my school, St Bede's Catholic High in Ormskirk, like a football team.

The experience of working with the people we spoke to for this book has given me a clear understanding of what is required for improved organisational performance.

As a result, our school has seen academic performance improve across year groups, a restructured leadership team, much improved public relations with key stakeholders in the community and parent body, increased staff wellbeing, more focus on student voices, an improved careers programme and the development of many colleagues at all levels, which has resulted in internal and external promotions for them.

As for Micky, writing this book has been a labour of love. He is driven by a passion not only to improve himself but to help others. He told me: 'I'd read these books on 90-day business plans and I understood what they were trying to say but I didn't really feel it. I wanted to hear the stories of the people who have lived it. Then I thought, there's never been a book like this written about football managers.

'We are masters of this 100 days, well, those of us still in a job. I want to see fewer managers get the sack. We watched new managers like hawks in their first 100 days. Some of them we've thought must be really clever. Others we've seen make massive mistakes in the press or with the supporters and we've known that they just haven't been prepared properly. I hope this book starts to help managers like me to have a better chance of winning hearts, minds and matches.'

Micky vehemently believes that the process of writing this book has made him a better manager and refined his approach to his leadership of a football team.

As we came to complete the writing, Micky had moved from Tranmere Rovers to Dundee United. Micky is now leading a Premier League side in his home country of Scotland and has the opportunity he richly deserves following many years of success in lower league English football. He credits his recent development to the lessons we have learnt through the writing of this book.

Leadership secrets of the Premier League bosses

Many of those lessons we both learnt were from some of the biggest names in the game. You will read the incredible story of how the popular but unfancied new interim manager at Old Trafford, Ole Gunnar Solskjær, secured his and many managers' dream job in exactly 100 days.

You will read inside stories from Manchester United about his key decisions, cultural changes and unassuming style which realigned a fractured culture. You will sit with Ole, Micky, Mick Phelan and I at Carrington, the club's training ground, as Ole opens his first '100 days diary' and tells us the whole story.

You will also read about the business-like brain of Sam Allardyce. You will sit in Big Sam's living room while he talks through the systematic way he turns around the behaviours, culture and performance of teams who seemed to be dead and buried in the Premier League's relegation zone. It is no accident. Sam's approach is a tried and tested model for turnarounds that can be applied to businesses, schools, football teams and any other organisation you care to mention.

We will go inside the mind of Sean Dyche while sat in his training ground office. Another unfancied and unpopular choice of manager when he first took the reins at Burnley Football Club, Dyche's approach has created a commitment culture and driven a club to overperform for many years in the Premier League. This success was based on decisions which improved the team's performance, organisational alignment and team identity. Dyche also talks of managing stress and wellbeing through a combination of humility and grit.

Another Premier League manager, David Moyes, will reveal his personal approach to the most testing of football situations and will explain how he has fine-tuned his management technique over time, and a fellow former Everton boss, Joe Royle, will tell us the vital importance of embracing history and culture as you take your place at the helm of a grand old team searching for identity and new direction. Former Arsenal and Scotland women's football manager Shelley Kerr will discuss her experience of managing relationships and the critical importance of getting recruitment right.

To combine insights of sport and business, Mark Palios spoke to us at length about his work at the Football Association as the Chief Executive, at PricewaterhouseCoopers as Senior Partner and as football club chairman at Tranmere Rovers.

And this book is also punctuated by the insights of Drew Povey, a leadership coach who has worked with companies such as Rolls-Royce, Lloyds Banks, England Rugby Union & Greater Manchester Police.

Among other voices who some of you may not have come across before is Tuesday Humby, who turned around a failing school to become one of the country's top performers, and leading speaker and best-selling author, Paul McGee, who offers a great deal of insight into the world of personal care and wellbeing.

Finally, we have read a lot of research around this subject. The opinions, models, approaches and successes of these managers will be supported by evidence that explains why some people win and some people lose within those first 100 days. The psychology, sociology and sometimes simple statistics of success can reveal as much as the expert voices we have in this book.

Micky and I have written this book in order that we can help people in football, business, education and life. The lessons that both of us learnt during the process led us both to successful outcomes in our leadership roles. Now, we would like you to read about, enjoy and learn from these lessons too.

This is the story of that incredible journey which we would start at the home of one of the world's most famous football clubs.

Phil Denton, 2021

Chapter One

THE MONTH BEFORE DAY 1

 Understanding the challenge ahead

You know the club. Make them smile

'We came in just before Christmas. I suppose it was like coming in on loan. I was given a six-month contract as caretaker manager. Our instruction was to finish the season and then I was going to go back to Molde. It wasn't like, 'Come in and change the club and put your stamp on it.' It was, 'come in; you know the club, you know the expectations, make them smile, play attacking football and give youth a chance.'

This was the message from Ed Woodward, the Chief Executive of Manchester United, on Tuesday, December 18th, 2018 when he contacted Ole Gunnar Solskjær and asked him to undertake the leadership role in one of the biggest clubs in the world. With that, the biggest 100 days in Ole's managerial career began and it would be exactly 100 days later that his fate would be decided.

His is the first of many case studies you will hear of that

illustrates the critical actions leaders can take in order to get off to the strongest possible start.

Micky and I travelled to meet Ole on a crisp, winter's afternoon. We followed the path that Ole would have taken on his first day, beyond a barrier and down a non-descript road that takes you to United's famous training ground, Carrington. A road that had been travelled by greats such as Beckham, Cantona, Ronaldo and Rooney.

As you enter the complex car park, you are greeted with a vision and aura of excellence. Micky led me to the walkway that links the academy training centre to the first team complex. Underneath a wave-like, clear glass canopy, is a water feature and the names of all the successful academy graduates etched into glass panels. We picked out names we recognised from the near and distant past. Some of the game's greats are celebrated right there. Perhaps as importantly as that, some names of players that may have made the initial jump but then fallen by the wayside are also captured to remind any graduates that their work has only just begun.

As you enter that first team training centre, you are greeted by Kath. Kath has been sitting at that desk, or several iterations of it, for 51 years. She has seen them all she told us, 'From Sir Bobby Charlton to Ronaldo...', they've all walked past her and no doubt enjoyed the steely Mancunian humour that is mixed in equal measure with her genuinely warm and caring welcome. We signed ourselves in and took our seat, waiting for Ole and Mick Phelan, his number two. This was the first illustration of perhaps a surprising element of the United culture. This is a family club. This is a proud club. This is a club with a rugged, industrial determination to represent the city of Manchester properly. That said, as Ole would later explain, it was a context that his predecessors had potentially misread.

After a few minutes, Ole and Mick came to the reception to meet us. They did not send a secretary down, they didn't call down and have us sent up, they came and shook our hands and asked us how we were. Immediately, we could see why Ole and Mick had the impact they had when they arrived at United. They understood this place uniquely. They were the living, breathing embodiment of the culture. They exuded it because they understood it. The first lesson of this book is that you need to get to grips with the culture and history of your team before you walk in the door on Day 1 or as quickly as possible thereafter.

As you walk towards the manager's office, you walk past European Cups, UEFA Cups, FA Cups and the Premier League trophy. You expect all of that in a way, but what made an instant impact for me was the way that Ole would not let anyone hold the door for him; he held the door for us and took us to get a coffee, which he made before we sat down in the office to begin our interview.

In the first 100 days, words are really important, but actions are even more significant. We could see immediately why smiles had been brought back to Manchester United. Our first question was if Ole and Mick actually realised how they had transformed a club from a beleaguered old ship back to a modern, evolving version of its glorious past.

Later on, we will return to Ole and Mick to discover what they believe was the key to unlocking the United revival. The first lesson for us was that before a manager walks through the door on Day 1, they need to be ready for the challenge ahead. Arguably, this is even more important for a leader that walks into a failing environment. Our next managerial legend, with a reputation for turning failing teams around is Sam Allardyce. The ex-Premier League and England national team manager shared his expert knowledge of what it takes to get off to a winning start in leadership.

The importance of being prepared

Allardyce, affectionately known as 'Big Sam' by football fans and the British media, is a past master at getting his homework right and rapidly changing the efficiency of a football team.

'There's no doubt that your first 100 days are the most important as a manager. No doubt at all about that. You've just got to get it right. That means making sure you use your time effectively to make accurate judgements about the players, the staff, the fans and the board. Then you've got to get your stamp on the place quickly but it can't just be the same stamp you used at the last place,' he told us.

Allardyce sat relaxed in the armchair of his living room after walking from the kitchen with a cold drink he had just poured. Micky sat on the couch, talking to his ex-manager and now his quasi-mentor. The two had developed a relationship based on mutual respect not just through their football and managerial acumen but also their characters.

They both know the value of hard work and instil that value within the teams and clubs they have led. Whenever Micky's name is mentioned on national radio, Sam is the first to revere his achievements. It was due to that respect and trust that Sam shared with us his thoughts, beliefs and experiences in a more candid way than he has perhaps ever done before publicly.

We all face transition points in work and life. Sam appears adept at using his transition points to propel Premier League teams from points of despair to elation. Examples of these incredible transitions have been seen at Sunderland, Crystal Palace and Everton to name but a few. But they are not straightforward or simple things to navigate. In fact, such is the challenge of transition points and dangerous situations that they are analysed by the US Army War College using the acronym VUCA.

The new football manager faces a dangerous situation like no other. Their career and reputation is on the line from minute one. 'It's like drinking from a fire hose. You're just bombarded with information that you need to process quickly or you'll be caught out,' says Allardyce.

Like successful football managers, the US military knows that the volatility of a transition or situation such as the first 100 days is guaranteed and so they prepare for these VUCA circumstances. The acronym points to four components of any transitional period; volatility, uncertainty, complexity and ambiguity. To decipher these four elements is to begin your first 100 days by getting under the skin of any new challenge.

The American Military employed the term VUCA to encapsulate the extreme conditions they encountered in Iraq and Afghanistan after the second Gulf War. Taking over the leadership of a football club's fortunes plunges individuals, many of whom were simply good players, into a VUCA world which they must quickly untangle. In order to succeed in a VUCA world, leaders must retain vision, offer clear strategy, anticipate challenges, embrace the complexity, reduce the ambiguity and embed a culture and key principles designed to withstanding the volatility of a financial year or football season.

Challenging the complexity

'You've got to understand what you're walking into,' explained Sam as he sat back in his chair. 'Before you walk in that building you need to get your hands on as much information as possible so that you can be best prepared. You can find out about the financial position, the owners, the players, the staff, the fans and recent history. You'll need all of that to best prepare yourself for making your first 100 days a success. Whatever type of leader you are, being prepared is key.'

As the famous saying goes: 'If you always do what you've always done, then you'll always get what you've always got.' Right? Wrong! There are countless stories and examples of leaders who entered into new roles with the view that worked before will work again. Allardyce has a long history of club success. He cites not revising his approach in the early part of his career as one of his quickest learning curves.

'I'd done really well at Bolton. We had some great years. We had a way of preparing, playing and recruiting that got us in to European competitions on a small budget. We recruited some of the most exciting players in the league at the time and people were shocked by some of the big names coming to Bolton. Then I got the Newcastle job and so I went up there thinking I had the winning formula. It didn't work, it was a different place and then there was a takeover which no-one saw coming. I learnt from that experience that you do need to tailor your approach based on the club you're walking into.'

Allardyce uses a STARS model as referred to in a book called 'The First 90 Days' by Michael D. Watkins. The STARS model (below) helps Allardyce define his approach for effectively assessing the current state of a football club. Understanding the STARS model also helps the new leader, while in transition, understand what style of leadership is required for the situation. Understanding the club, team, department or company allows the leader to apply the most appropriate strategy.

STARS model of organisational planning

START UP	TURNAROUND	ACCELERATED GROWTH

REALIGNMENT	SUSTAINED GROWTH

Allardyce puts this business philosophy into a football context, 'In football, like in business, leaders have to work with managers, owners, CEOs that will often have ambitious expectations for the first 100 days in the role. The position of manager will often have become vacant due to the failure of the previous manager to meet the expectations of the owner. Beyond the owner, expectations can be set by supporters, shareholders, the media and anyone else who cares to pass comment and is listened to. The best managers and leaders are really clever in the way they handle this expectation because they understand and communicate the starting point well.'

During the global pandemic, getting an understanding of the organisation you are entering is perhaps even more crucial. After all, it may well have changed significantly due to the impact of the health crisis and subsequent financial devastation. Let's explore this STARS model now. You can consider where your team, office, school or business currently sits on this continuum.

The components of the STARS model:

Start-Up – Love what you are selling

The business world is littered with start-ups that fail more than they succeed. Successful start-ups all come from embryonic beginnings and achieve rapid growth through an array of factors. Start-ups require the recruitment of highly skilled, motivated people who are committed to a shared vision which is the core purpose of the organisation.

Austin MacPhee merges sport and business leadership. He began two start-up companies. The first is AMsoccer, a charity in his local community which delivers coaching programmes ranging from classes for youngsters aged 3+ to walking football where over-80s play. The charity club has regularly seen young players graduate through the year groups and earn opportunities to progress in the professional game. The second start-up is AM Sports Tours Limited. This company delivers football tours worldwide with offices in the USA, a turnover of more than £2 million a year and tour programmes to over 30 countries worldwide.

Between the charity and company, he employs many local people and it is integral to the local sporting community. Austin is also assistant coach for the Northern Ireland national side having been by Michael O'Neill's side for more than 63 international games. He has been assistant and interim manager in the Scottish Premier League and remarkably started in amateur football just 12 years ago.

His advice on using his sports leadership knowledge with creating a successful start-up was simple and stepped: 'Make sure you love the thing that your business will try to sell. It helps if you can speak through personal experience and have lived it. For me, I knew football and I knew football tours internationally. I have played in football professionally and semi-professionally in Scotland, Japan, Romania and the USA. As a kid, I'd been on these tours and knew the value they had for me, so I believed in it. It is authentic if you have lived it'.

With a clear passion demonstrated, Austin then explained

how start-ups go about getting their foot on the business ladder. 'You need to sell that idea to your first customer and, crucially, you need to retain them as this gives you momentum for growth. Once you've done that, gather the right people around you and learn from people who believe in what you do but have different experience. Once you've got that momentum, speak with confidence, practise it. You'll need that skill when you're getting more customers or getting money from the bank. Planning is important but don't over-think things and just start getting out there to 'do'. This is vital as you need customers quickly unless you have significant investment behind you. Plans can be too long-term at times, especially at the start.'

Start-ups are faced with challenges of establishing a culture and identity amongst the players and staff. As Austin continued: 'When you expand you've got to give a bit of your baby away. The people you bring in have got to feel like this is their company as well now. That's a real similarity to a manager building his coaching team around him. Young managers often want to do everything themselves, but as they gather experience and the right staff they start to give a bit of their week away!'

Externally, the challenge for the leader is to create that identity amongst the community. 'I did this through getting into schools, free local tournaments and supporting local causes when establishing AMsoccer in North East Fife,' explained Austin.

Start-ups in English football have included MK Dons and AFC Wimbledon. Leaders at these clubs face the unique aforementioned challenges – however they also have the chance to set the culture at the club for the modern game and for the modern supporters. They are arguably not beset with the frustrations of the past or a heavy weight of expectation for the future.

Turnaround – Operation Sam

Due to the high turnover of managers in the game, this is perhaps the most common scenario for new managers in football to find themselves in. Turnaround situations usually occur when a team has been performing poorly which has resulted in the sacking of the manager.

Sam Allardyce has often been described as a manager who 'does what it says on the tin!' when drafted in to situations where a team is struggling in the lower echelons of the English Premier League. The reference does not do justice to a manager who has ensured the Premier League survival of Bolton Wanderers, West Ham United, Sunderland, Crystal Palace and Everton. All five clubs were either exceeding expectations given the support base and resources, or falling short of the demands of owners and supporters for the same reasons.

Allardyce brings structure, stability and intelligence to the situations which has seen him repeatedly succeed. 'From Day 1 it's important to lead the rest of the staff and establish trust by explaining exactly what you expect from them. I like to bring my own men in who become my eyes and ears around the place. What you can usually guarantee is that when a new manager comes in, you'll get a positive reaction.

The players will want to win games of football for you and you need to try and ride on the crest of that wave for as long as possible. While you're doing that you need to be finding out what the real problems are because they have not gone away but what you do get with some early success is time to find out.

'In any turnaround situation, you need to offer the light at the end of the tunnel to create a sense of hope. In football, I give this not with a vision of words but a vision of really simple actions. The actions are on the training pitch and they mean, if the players do what we ask, they will improve their performances. You can't say they'll improve results, they usually do, but you can say they'll help you concede fewer goals, create more chances and improve your stats across the pitch. You also can improve the way the players eat, recover and generally live while they're in the building.'

Allardyce continued: 'Whatever type of organisation it is, if you're turning something around you need to be quick, clear and consistent. All the while you know that the short-term reaction won't last, so you've got to find those long-term fixes that need to be made in the background. That might be your staffing structure or finances, they need to be sorted when you've got confidence from those around you because the turnaround is happening.'

Through this approach, Sam gains an understanding of what needs to be improved long-term while the short-term is improved under what we will call 'Operation Sam'.

In spheres such as business and education the very same situations exist. Leaders undertake companies or schools with a poor recent record, low morale of staff and a feeling of impending doom. Leaders in such situations can take much from the approach of Allardyce.

Throughout this book we will look at examples of highly successful leaders in the world of football and beyond. One such leader, who had an astonishing turnaround success story is Tuesday Humby who is the Executive Principle and Regional Director for Ormiston Academies. Tuesday transformed a failing school which was unpopular and riddled with behavioural issues to become one of the highest performing schools in the country. Tuesday took the same approach as Allardyce in focusing on one key aspect of performance and introducing a tried and tested technique to improve it.

In Tuesday's case it was not keeping 'clean sheets' but rather directing the teachers to teach in a systematic way which would improve learning, behaviour and academic outcomes. Like Allardyce, the message was simple from Tuesday: 'If you teach like this, with these principles, then the behaviour, learning and outcomes of your classes will improve.' As we will discuss, such a directive approach is not appropriate in all situations but both Tuesday and Big Sam have recognised, through experience, that in turnaround situations when time is of a premium, quick and effective action must be taken to ensure rapid gains.

The global pandemic has perhaps brought about a new type of turnaround situation. Changing a situation which is all too unclear and bringing clarity. As with everything, Micky is measured about such a scenario. 'You need to approach uncertainty with patience. Let it come to you and then use the skills that you have developed, you'll know how to deal with it. I'm not saying be complacent at all but just give yourself the time to get an understanding of the situation before rushing in.'

Accelerated Growth – Bolton in Europe

In the book 'Good To Great' Jim Collins highlights personal humility and professional will as qualities needed to take an organisation to the next level. Collins describes these characteristics as being underpinned by an individual who 'looks in the mirror, not out of the window, to apportion responsibility for poor results…' while also looking 'out of the window, not in the mirror, to apportion credit for the success of the company'.

Sam Allardyce was looking firmly out of the window when he took the reins at Bolton Wanderers in 2003. Allardyce succeeded Colin Todd, who was well respected and only left in protest following the sale of a top player. Allardyce had impressed with his ability to create a great team that was greater than the sum of its parts. He accelerated the club's growth through the implementation of a revised recruitment policy which involved buying players just past their best but capable of outstanding contributions for the Lancastrian side. He was perhaps pioneering in his financial prowess as he did not have large funds for transfer fees at his disposal and so he spent money on the wages he could recruit for small fees or free transfers.

The changes were targeted marginal gains which applied

pragmatism and logic rather than the romantic and often 'gung-ho' approach of many football club owners and managers desperate for success. The defining success for Allardyce happened at the end of the 2004–2005 season when Bolton defeated Everton on the last day of the season to qualify for European football.

The team that defeated Everton contained Vicent Candela (31), Bruno N'Gotty (33), Fernando Hierro (37) Stelios Giannakopoulos (30), Jay-Jay Okocha (31) and Gary Speed (35). Allardyce had accelerated growth through calculated investments and looking out of the window, scouring Europe and every possible analytical model to find the edge that Bolton required. Accelerating growth requires such an approach that balances the improvement of standard operations and an innovation which allows for large jumps in a team's effectiveness.

Realignment – Why?

When Micky took on Tranmere Rovers he returned a 'why?' to the club. He ignited the supporters because he understood them and they understood him.

Micky explains: 'I told the players, the fans and everyone connected with the club that they were right to expect Tranmere to win games. I told them that the people of the Wirral and of Birkenhead deserved to have their hometown team winning and making them proud.

'People had lost hope and belief in what the club stood for. I told the players that this club stood for hard work, working class people, pride in endeavour and it has an incredible history. I told them all this because I believe that is true and I told them it again, and again and again until we all started saying it and people started believing it. You bring people together and you can accomplish anything. The important thing for me is you recognise why this club or business existed in the first place and you bring people back to that when things have gone wrong.'

To refocus a team, organisation or department requires an acknowledgement of the core purpose. Business guru and author Simon Sinek implores all leaders to 'Start with Why' in the book of the same title. Sinek explored successful businesses such as Apple and explained how Apple starts with its purpose, or its *why*, and works out from there.

This is graphically illustrated in his 'Golden Circle' (below). This simple, but globally recognised model focusses the leader on basing all actions on *why* rather than *how* or *what*.

We will explore the concept of vision in Chapter 4 but for the purpose of a realignment task it is important to begin with an approach that fosters cohesion and a common purpose which must be centred on a 'why'.

The Golden Circle

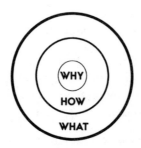

Sustaining success – Shelley's Arsenal

The job of sustaining success is a rare one in football as most positions become available due to a poor run of results for the previous incumbent. I spoke with a manager who had to contend with such a challenge. Shelley Kerr is one of the highest-profile managers in the women's game in Britain. Shelley gave up an afternoon to chat with me from her home in Scotland. We shared a video call over cups of tea to the tune of her dog barking in the background and talked about how she has developed as a leader, especially in those first 100 days.

Shelley, or Michelle Kerr, had a very successful playing career during which she won every domestic honour in Scotland and played in the UEFA Women's Cup (now the UEFA Champions League). She also represented her country in UEFA and FIFA qualification campaigns. This led to a ground-breaking managerial career that saw her take the reins at Arsenal Ladies in 2013, winning the FA Cup twice. She then made national news when she became the first female manager in British men's senior football after being appointed manager of Stirling University, competing in the Lowland League.

After three successful years in Stirling, Shelley was appointed head coach of the Scotland women's national team. She was the first person to lead the side to the FIFA Women's World Cup in 2019. As well as the many honours she has earned in football, she was also recognised in the 2019 Queen's Birthday Honours List for services to football.

Shelley has had two major managerial jobs, the first being Arsenal Ladies with the second being the Scotland national job. It was the former where Shelley took on a role that required an approach fit to sustain success. In order to sustain success, Shelley built on strengths and found marginal gains across the organisation. She explained the situation as she arrived at Arsenal.

'We had a group of players who had been very successful but a squad that was coming towards the end of their careers. We also needed to prepare for the club turning professional. I knew we had some strategic and infrastructure things we had to do with limited resources, along with challenges of recruitment. In women's football, you always need to get a link with the club to get more resources. I was mindful of these things but in the meantime I still had the expectations of being one of the best teams in Europe and needing to win!' Externally, this would appear a sustaining success job, however there were many elements that required turnaround and some that could even be considered start-up.

At Arsenal, Shelley immediately began to gain an under-standing of the players before looking at other areas of the club. This was because, as she explained, she realised that results on the pitch were her initial priority before she could address longer-term development goals. 'I was experienced as a coach at this point so I knew I could help improve the players, regardless of their experience and success. Also, being out there on the training pitch, you get a clearer idea of what you need to do recruitment wise.

'I got to know the club. It had a winning culture that had

already been created so I didn't want to change too much. I wanted to keep it consistent in terms of a possession-based style which is synonymous with Arsenal.'

Despite the eagerness to sustain the winning formula at the club, Shelley began to explain just how she had brought in her own rigorous and systematic process of developing teams and systems. Humble as ever, she explained: 'I tried to instil some kind of consistency for team meetings. We had a framework for coaching and development in the club. I also worked hard to manage the expectations of stakeholders inside and outside of the club. I relied on key personnel at the club already there. I spoke with senior players, you have to have trust them. My communication with these key people was really important.

'I also spoke a lot with the general manager who was also important at the club. I spoke a lot with them about where I felt the club should be going in terms of the move from amateur to semi-pro to professional.' These were quick wins that allowed her to stamp her approach on the team in a way that cultivated a proud recent history and looked to a driven bright future. She judged this approach perfectly by spending time asking and listening before seeing where she could add value to the organisation.

Crucially, Shelley stresses that she is always aware she does not have all the answers and that she is only one player in a much wider team effort. She described how she gathers external input. 'I have had mentors throughout my career, often from outside of football. I go through scenarios with them like strategic planning. It's really important to get a neutral viewpoint.' It clearly had a successful effect as in Shelley's first season, Arsenal won the FA Cup, the League Cup and they reached the semi-final of the Champions League. Shelley found the marginal gains to sustain success through her experience, humility and a strong support network.

Negotiating success – lay down the goalposts

Once the start point has been established for the leadership role, the manager must negotiate what success will look like. This should look something like a SMART (Specific, Measurable, Attainable, Realistic and Timed) goal. The negotiation can take place with a CEO, board of directors, line manager or, in this case, a football club owner.

Tranmere Rovers is a medium-sized football club that had tumbled down the divisions for more than a decade alongside an almost physical rotting of the infrastructure. The memories of promotions, cup glory and iconic players weighed like an anchor on the players who could not fulfil the expectations of downtrodden supporters. The support base had halved, the income had plummeted and the hopes for the future were fading like the blue paint on the main stand. The fall had been so great that the club now languished in non-league and sat 10th in the league table.

There had been a succession of managerial appointments who could not deliver the success the passionate supporters and dedicated club hierarchy craved. Then, owner and chairman, ex- FA Chief Executive Mark Palios, made a call to former player Micky Mellon. Palios had just dismissed the previous manager Gary Brabin who, in his first season, had done a great job in stopping the rot on the field and recruiting some quality players. However, after a strong start initially, a poor run of results during the start of his second season had led to Palios feeling a change was necessary to achieve promotion back into the Football League.

At the time, Micky was a manager at Shrewsbury in League One, two divisions above Rovers. He also had a track record of success following several promotions with both Shrewsbury and Fleetwood. Now an experienced manager, Micky travelled to meet Palios to discuss the role with an open mind but a healthy dose of reality which football management serves by the bucketful.

During the initial phone call, Micky recalls: 'I asked Mark if he would like a presentation. I think he said 'yes' so I replied that was fine because I could get a marketing company to produce the finest presentation, the video analyst could highlight the style of play I would love to play and I could blow his head off with false promises. So then he just asked me to come along and talk through what I thought I could do at the club.

'This is a key point in the build-up to your first 100 days. You've got to negotiate what success is and how you'll behave towards your boss from the first moment. I was in a strong position because I knew I'd be ok for management offers but still, even for the new manager, you've got to make sure that you get off on the right foot. That doesn't mean banging the table with ridiculous demands but you've got to say what you want things to be like. That goes for both sides of the boardroom table, the manager and the chairman or the employer and the employee. You're making sure that you get the ground rules sorted so you've some shared and realistic understanding of what success is going to look like. You can then remind your chairman of what you agreed when times get tough because, be assured, at some point they will.'

The physical goalposts on any football pitch do not move during the game. The metaphoric goalposts seen by supporters, owners, players and media commentators can fluctuate frequently if they are not cemented in with an agreed success criteria discussed at the outset. Early season form can often raise expectations for the rank outsiders who shoot to the top with early successes. The expectations, hopes and dreams of fans can rise as quickly as they can fall once the reality of a long hard campaign sets in. Paradoxically, a long-term project to develop the culture and playing style of a club can create frustration amongst those emotionally invested in it if this was not the shared view at the manager's appointment. Therefore, negotiating the benchmarks for success or laying down the goalposts for the first 100 days is crucial to ensure leaders and their managers view this period with a healthy perspective.

Before entering a football club, Sam Allardyce has important questions he needs to ask in order to negotiate success. 'I like to sit down with the owner but this can be difficult in modern football. I get alarm bells if the owners don't want to meet the man who will be running their club but sometimes that is just the way things are in modern football. Whoever I meet, I get some things agreed and even, if possible, written into the contract. I ask what they expect of me and by when. You've got to negotiate this sometimes and try to be realistic because your chairman or boss of any sort might not be an expert in football or your field. Sometimes you need to educate them as to what is possible. Your owner might be saying 'Champions League qualification' when you're thinking 'survival in the league'! The thing with this is it applies to any walk of life. If you've got a boss in a factory who's moved up from engineering, he might know nothing about sales which you're involved in. So, in football and in any business you've got to negotiate your success before you even start.'

Allardyce follows by turning the table and then asking how the board or owner will support him in this quest. 'A club's finances are fairly accessible through the Deloitte accountancy agency and so it is possible to see where that club sits in terms of a budget league table. Statistically, the team with the biggest budget wins the league. The team with the smallest budget finishes last and so on. So if you're sitting across the table from the owner and he's saying 'finish top seven' then you need to be saying what budget you'll need to be able to do that. If they're not going to give you that budget then you need to be saying how difficult the task is going to be. That relationship with the owner needs to be all about honesty and trust. If you haven't got that then what hope have you got?'

At Tranmere, Micky and Mark Palios sat across the table from each other. Mark asked Micky: 'So, what can you do for Tranmere Rovers?' Micky recalls preparing for a question like this and he responded quickly: 'What do you want?' Palios was straightforward in his desire with one word: 'Promotion'. Rovers were 10th in the league with a side that were lacking in confidence, consistency and, arguably, the quality to mount a title challenge. With that in mind, Micky forced the issue of this negotiation by highlighting the aforementioned obstacles and asking: 'So, what will you do to allow me to do this?' Micky explains: 'Mark was taken aback at first I think but you've just got to be honest, otherwise you'll both end up disappointed. We were 10th and the team wasn't good enough to achieve what the chairman wanted. You get those tough conversations done early on in a proper, professional way and you can both move forward for the good of everyone in the building. I don't care what kind of leader you are; you've got to have the right resources to do the job or you're struggling from the get-go.'

The clarification of the expectations of those around us is essential. The discussions between your new boss – in a football sense, the owner and you – can be pivotal to your success. For Micky, this is initially centred around the resources available to him and culture around the club. The latter involved a series of seemingly small matters but ones which create early wins and momentum. The training kit was dated and of poor quality. Players wore different tops from seasons gone by. 'We got all that old training kit and we binned it. This was a new era now for me and for everyone connected with the club.' Micky insisted new training wear was ordered and it was. Micky didn't stop with the training attire. 'The door to my office creaked as it opened and it opened in a way that made it difficult for me to see players arrive or for them to see me. The frame and door were replaced. It wasn't just the door, it was the people in the building seeing that things were changing for the better. The training pitch had divots from the day before. I asked the groundsman if that was good enough. Now you've got him doing his job properly and the staff seeing what my standards are from my actions not just my words.'

Crucially, Micky went on to negotiate with the key personnel that ultimately dictate the success of any manager in his first 100 days, the players.

At an early training session Micky led following a week of closely observing the habits and culture of the side, he had one key question: 'What do you want to achieve?'

'The team gave me a range of responses that went from styles of play, levels of fitness and pleasing the fans. I asked: How about promotion?' It is a question that can result in only one answer. Of course, the squad responded affirmatively and then the criteria by which all standards were measured was set. 'I got them to say to me: 'Treat me like a champion.' Now they'd said that, I knew I could get the very best out of these lads. This includes the way we train, the way we recover and our attitude around the place. The players were united in their desire for this to be the case because they knew that nothing else would be enough'.

Instantly, Micky had the licence, given to him by the owner and now agreed to by the players, that only the highest of performances, attitudes and output would be accepted because that is what would be required. Success had been negotiated. It had been agreed. The culture had been set. Now came time for the next steps to utilise this mandate to drive standards across the club.

Mark Palios – the Turnaround Guru

Mark Palios didn't follow the usual path of a footballer when his career finished. He developed a successful career as a chartered accountant and ultimately became a senior partner in a big-name company, specialising in business turnaround. After winning a top finance award in 2003 – Turnaround Financier of the Year and picking up a Lifetime Achievement Award – he went on to become the Football Association's Chief Executive. One of his priority tasks was to stabilise The FA's perilous financial situation, by resolving the financing of the Wembley Stadium project. By saving The FA hundreds of millions of pounds, he is reported to have safeguarded the future of the organisation.

Palios is in no doubt about the importance of the first 100 days, 'This is the most important period as a leader because you set the tone for the rest of your time in the business. What you can't get drawn into is being swept away with the 'something has got to be done' brigade. You must take your time and see things for yourself. If you jump in making decisions, you can live to regret it. I start off looking at three commodities. There's only one you can't get more of. There's people, money and time. You can always get more money, more people but you can never get more time.

Now chairman of Tranmere Rovers, Micky and I sat with Palios in his office one night in late August. Across the desk there were papers detailing plans, finance and reports that reflected the fine attention to detail and meticulous planning that had been the framework for two back to back promotion-winning seasons.

Over the course of many hours, Mark would give us the business dynamic for an effective 100 days that took our voyage of discovery to another level. He sat relaxed, sipping a black filtered coffee and occasionally flashing a glance towards his large office whiteboard. The board had an array of scribbles that detailed immediate priorities, long-term goals and an insight into the ultimate vision for this resurgent football club. Palios gave us the language we craved which would pull together the thinking of great footballing minds, business leaders and educationalists.

Palios explained: 'In the first 100 days, I go straight to the HR manager to find out who's who and what's what. Then I look at the finances to see what is possible. Finally, I see the time. I consider timeframes and when things will need to be done by. People, time and money, it's the triangle you need to get to grips with quickly. If you've not got a real understanding of that then you can make uninformed decisions that affect your credibility internally and externally.'

Micky asked Mark whether he goes in with preconceived priorities. Palios replies: 'My priority is to get under the skin of the place. Once you understand those three elements, you can start to set out your plans for turnaround.'

In a 30-year career, he led business turnarounds for

approximately 1,000 companies by his estimation. These experiences have allowed him to develop a tried and tested toolkit for leading rapid change within his first 100 days in post.

The Palios Turnaround Triangle

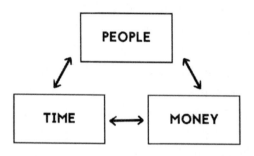

The companies and organisations Palios would be involved with were on the brink of collapse and many had suffered years of decline due to a wide range of factors. The FA was no different. Palios said: 'You may well not be an industry expert, but you become a situational expert. That situation is often a turnaround within the all-important first 100 days – the crucial thing you need to establish across an organisation is credibility.'

This word, credibility, quickly became a theme that he would return to repeatedly. It's a word and concept of leadership that we had yet to explore or even really consider. Within the first days of any leader's tenure, Palios was adamant that, '…proving your credibility as an individual and the organisation's credibility is fundamental to every decision and action. Without it, you're sunk!'

Final countdown

Micky and I had already been talking a lot over the phone and in person. At times I was just trying to take on board the wealth of knowledge he was sharing with me from his experiences of walking into a club for the first time. The time to begin my headship role was just days away.

So far I had taken on board the importance of understanding the situation and reducing the unknowns so I could adjust my approach and my message accordingly. Now, as my blast-off to a career as a headteacher was just days away, Micky set about sharing with me the final few pieces of the preparation jig-saw that would help me be ready for the first day in my own version of the dugout.

So far, I had assessed the headship of St Bede's as largely being a role that required an approach in line with sustaining success but, as I would discover in the final days before I took over, there was a good deal of realignment to tackle as well. One thing was for sure, this journey had only just begun and I was realising how little I knew about making sure I was going to get off to a winning start.

Reflections

1. Gathering all available information, how would you assess the situation of your new role using the VUCA approach (i.e. volatility, uncertainty, complexity and ambiguity)?

2. What will the success criteria be and how will you ensure that the person you report to is aware and agrees to the parameters?

3. How will you communicate the negotiated success criteria across the organisation?

4. What will the expectations be in order to achieve this negotiated success?

5. When will the methods being employed be reviewed and scrutinised?

6. How will you find out what situation you are walking into?

7. In what ways will that affect your approach?

8. What will you do in the week before you take over to make sure you get off to a winning start?

Chapter Two

THE WEEK BEFORE DAY 1

| | Setting up to win | |

Why you?

Micky believes that any manager or leader must understand how they 'fit' within a club or organisation. What you have to think about as you're getting ready to get hold of your team or new leadership role is *why you?* Any leader must understand what the qualities are that have brought them to this point.

As we sat with Ole Gunnar Solskjær and Mick Phelan at Manchester United's training ground in Carrington, we asked if Ole knew why he was chosen to lead United into their next chapter. 'I think it was me because I knew the club. Ed (Woodward) had been following me in Molde (the Norwegian side where Solskjær had achieved much success). The 'manager' (Sir Alex) and David Gill had approved of my personality coming in. It was never like, 'we want you to get us in the Champions League' said Ole. Mick (Phelan) added: 'I thought that it was about having Manchester

United people back running the club. In Ole's case, he was more about Man United, not about who was sat there at the top. We had a feel for the club and it wasn't really about us. We also understood the tradition here as well. Going back to Sir Matt Busby and even beyond that. You have to understand the tradition of this club which is industrial, hard graft and rolling your sleeves up. The ones who have been successful have embraced the tradition and culture here.' It was clear that in recent years, some of that had been lost. Both Ole and Mick were clear that their first priority was to reignite the culture and tradition of this world famous club. Both had a clear picture of why they were there, which really helped them to act accordingly.

Before Ole there had been a manager for 26 years in Sir Alex Ferguson. Since Sir Alex had retired there had been three managers in six years: David Moyes, Louis Van Gaal and José Mourinho.

Ole quickly assessed the situation he had inherited. 'It was a bit like going to Waitrose or Tesco. You spend 90 quid or 100 quid. Then you get home and try to make a meal but you've just got a bit of everything instead of what you need to make a good meal. When I arrived, some of the players had been here since Sir Alex, then David (Moyes) had signed a few, then Van Gaal signed a few, then Mourinho signed a few and they've all got different styles.'

The meal that Ole and Mick wanted to cook up did not have the ingredients they needed. That is not to say the ingredients or the previous chefs were at fault. Ryan Giggs, Wayne Rooney and Marcus Rashford have all said publicly how much they enjoyed working with Louis Van Gaal. Van Gaal ended his United reign after winning the FA Cup. José Mourinho won trophies with United and David Moyes was operating under very difficult circumstances after following the legend of Sir Alex Ferguson. However, Ole recognised that to achieve the cultural blend he desired on the pitch, he was not starting with the ingredients he needed.

'Our group had so many different strengths but not many were what we would think of as Manchester United players. These are players that have pace, power and personality. We're influenced by Sir Alex and that's what our opinion of a Manchester United player is.' For any new leader, understanding the leadership style that has gone before and the impact that this has had on the organisation is important.

Unlike many leadership roles, Ole didn't have the luxury of a month or even a week before he needed to be in the job and making a difference. 'I am a United fan so I had kept up to date with how they were playing because I watched them on TV. So much had changed, though, when I came back. I could write a list for you about the differences here,' he explained. They gave themselves time to absorb all the external information before arriving at the training ground.

In terms of their approach to this leadership role, the leadership duo decided that they would be themselves. Yes, they would speak of what it took to be a Manchester United player. They would share their experiences of what it took to be one of the most successful teams in the world. However, crucially, they imposed their own approach to this Manchester United blueprint created by Sir Alex Ferguson.

They recognised that much had changed and they had a group of players with a different mindset. They would quickly set about assessing who would be part of this realignment and turnaround for the short, medium and long-term.

Creating leaders on the pitch

It is common for leaders like Ole and Mick to undertake a SWOT analysis (i.e. strengths, weaknesses, opportunities and threats) upon taking up a leadership role. In a football sense this may well include a review of the squad, the facilities and the club infrastructure. In the previous chapter, Mark Palios defined these areas as: money, people and time. These factors will either reflect the strengths or weaknesses of a club or organisation's current position. However, what should be a focus and more important to a new incumbent is a focus on the future – the opportunities and threats.

Organisational SWOT Analysis

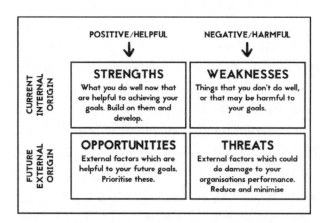

The Week Before Day 1

When Micky took over at Tranmere Rovers he was returning to a club for which he had much affinity. 'I had played for the club when they were challenging for the Premier League. We had great cup runs and the club even got to a League Cup final in 2000,' he said.

Before discussions with Mark Palios began, Micky called his friend 'Tranmere Tony' for a catch-up about life and, without giving the club's interest in him away, the state of Tranmere Rovers. 'Tony gave me chapter and verse about the reasons for the demise but the new waves of optimism which the supporters now had because of the owner's drive. I also gave the previous manager a call and he told me about the qualities in the squad and the fan base. I watched hours of matches, press conferences, I spoke to the groundsman and even got online to read what the fans were saying. It gave me a list of things that I could say were either opportunities to improve things or threats to the club.'

By the time he took his place in the dugout, Micky knew exactly what the fans needed to hear. He had developed a strategy to convey a new professionalism, a sense of belief and identity. Immediately, Micky achieved a cultural shift by talking about the club with the same reverence held firm by a loyal group of supporters that had maintained their support through the darkest of sporting times. There was no longer a focus on the past, of strengths and weaknesses. As Micky surveyed the club, he saw quick wins everywhere. There were opportunities at every point to make the players, supporters and all those connected with the club feel a renewed sense of hope and optimism.

Micky and I again discussed this approach over our hands-free phones on a commute to work one morning. I was a day away from beginning my first 100 days as head teacher at St Bede's. As I attempted to navigate the road works of the M62 from my home in Salford to my school in Lancashire, I explained to Micky the surprising results of the online staff survey I had conducted in order to gauge these opportunities and threats.

There was a professional frustration amongst many members of the team. Many of the staff were well capable of being senior leaders and they had a deep sense of loyalty to the school. 'You've got people wanting to lead and move things on,' Micky suggested, 'so get them to lead.' Micky gave me the example of working with his players to be part of the solution rather than just giving them a solution.

'I spoke to one of our forwards recently and asked him how we should play against our next opponent. They play with a back three and we might need to change our approach. So we sat down with a flip chart and pen. I knew they'd played against a back three before so we talked about what had worked. Then we agreed our plan together. I know now that they'll give 100 per cent to that plan because they came up with it. I'm creating leaders on the pitch.'

That one conversation changed my thought process on bringing about a cultural change. I realised that I needed the leaders in my school to tell me what they needed and wanted in order that I could make them feel a part of the solution to whatever problems we faced.

To that end, I started talking to people about their

thoughts. What amazed me in that first week is that my understanding of the teachers changed again. Firstly, I thought the staff body were harmonious, then I realised that wasn't quite right but then I saw that they were aligned with their ambitions and desire to feel a greater sense of collective ownership.

Once I got to this point, I could start making plans with a clearer understanding and the trust of a group that saw I had taken the time to get to grips with the situation. The approach I then took was tailored to the specific situation at St Bede's. Micky and I categorised this, tailored and specific approach to understand your organisation in the week before your 100 days, into three P's.

The three P's of Planning

Every club, company or organisation requires a specific approach which considers three P's (below).

The Three P's of Planning

PEOPLE	POSITION	PURPOSE
✗ Who will we be working with?	✗ Where is the club right now?	✗ Why are we here?
✗ Those at every level of the organisational hierarchy e.g. the manager, the owner, the sporting director, the players, the support staff, the media team etc.	✗ Identify the opportunities and threats which will either provide support or obstacles for the implementation of any plan	✗ Understand and communicate the fundamental reasons for which the football club or business exists. Then focus all effort and attention towards achieving the core purpose

Micky considers this plan closely, 'You've got to start with a really clear goal in mind. Then you've got to sell it to the players. Really, I am a salesman. I have these ideas and we have this shared goal that we establish, then it's my job to sell these ideas to the players. I might go about it in all sorts of ways, either one to one or in a group. Like any salesman, you sell the reason behind them buying into it before you sell the idea itself.'

Let's now explore these three P's.

Get people believing – United for change

To begin with, the plan must recognise the purpose or objective. For Ole Gunnar Solskjær, it was to win matches in the short-term and bring back a sense of joy to Manchester United. He also had the caveats of giving youth team players opportunities, bringing back an exciting style of play and creating a unity between the club and the fans once again.

Despite being given just six months to achieve this, Ole would bring about much of the change in the first 50 days which realigned supporters to the purpose of Manchester United. The change in atmosphere was rapid, of course helped by the series of matches won. However, as the weeks rolled on, Ole realised that he needed a longer-term plan to bring about a change in the personnel in order to improve the position of the club in relation to other top Premier League teams, such as Liverpool and Manchester City.

At St Bede's my objective was clarified from my first day as I set out to support the continued development of the school so that it could become '...a world class school for children that want to make the world a better place.' These words form our school vision, written large in every corridor in the school. I was able to follow Micky's example of benchmarking every factor of the school against this objective. Drew Povey, star of Educating Manchester, author and executive leadership coach, defines this process as the belief triangle.

Povey's Belief Triangle

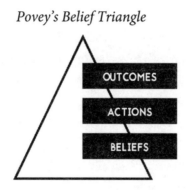

Drew met Micky and I to give us a perspective of his in-depth understanding of leadership in the worlds of business, sport and education. Following his nationally acclaimed leadership of Harrop Fold High School, Drew came to national attention as the star of the 'Educating Manchester' series. However, before this role, Drew spent a great deal of time working in elite sport. He was largely focused in Rugby League where he worked with the Warrington Wolves along with other professional clubs.

The television show and his best-selling books have now given Drew a global audience of leaders that are eager to learn from his user-friendly models. Micky and I were fascinated to hear Drew's approach to leadership, especially in preparing for transformational leadership within 100 days.

Drew explained: 'Within any organisation, team or school you have to affect people's beliefs if you really want to bring about change in their actions and then outcomes. It's the actions that you don't see that make the real difference. If you get that sort of effort by choice, your actions and then the outcomes are much more likely to be effective.

'You have to get people believing, though, in what you're trying to achieve. The first step to doing that is to start with the results. We have to be clear on what we want to get as an outcome. Then we need to explore the actions that will lead to that improvement in the results or outcomes.

'However, none of this can be achieved if the belief is not strong enough. Basically, beliefs shape our actions and actions deliver results.'

There is a common theme amongst the leaders spoken to during the writing of this book. Great football managers and leaders of all kinds, start with the end in mind and they are precise about what that end will look like. We will now explore how great leaders in the game have established that clarity from the outset, a clarity from the kick-off.

Will it make the boat go faster?

Continuing with the purpose theme, it is essential for a manager to establish a reason for decisions. When planning for a season, a training session or a game, it is important to think wholeheartedly about being successful in the moment.

Sam Allardyce explained: 'You've got to make sure that every player knows how important each game is. Sometimes they can get wrapped up in thinking that it's only the second game of the season so that game is not as important as the second-to-last game of the season. When you break your season down into sections then you realise just how vital every point is. Especially in the Premier League. I remember doing that at Bolton. We made it really clear that if we wanted to achieve our goals then we had to get those early wins against teams we knew we could beat. If we didn't, then we'd never get there at the end of the season. You've got to make sure you're making every training session, every meal and every game have a purpose.'

Objectives must be measurable and specific. It must be the epicentre for all strategy and actions that surround it. Ben Hunt-Davis and Harriet Beveridge's book entitled, 'Will It Make The Boat Go Faster?' charts the impact of a specific and measurable objective which became the mantra of the Great Britain rowing team.

After years of disappointment and glorious defeats, Ben Hunt-Davis and the GB Men's Rowing Eight won gold at the Sydney Olympics in 2000. The simple approach they took was to eliminate any action that would not improve their chance of winning or any action that would not 'make the boat go faster.' This mantra is written on our notice board at St Bede's. It is central to all of our decision making. If it won't make the boat go faster, then why bother doing it?

The objective must give those involved a sense of belief and ambition. It must draw together a team toward a goal that is something greater than they could achieve individually. It should be something which can be celebrated and accomplished in a manner which brings a collective and individual sense of purpose and reward.

Selling ideas – the 'Dogs of War'

To understand an organisation, you need to understand its people and the perception they have of that organisation's position. In exploring the next of the three P's, we spoke to Joe Royle, whose managerial career has taken him to Oldham Athletic, Everton, Manchester City and Ipswich.

From his home in West Lancashire, we spoke to Royle about the build-up to Day 1 because he has a track record of connecting with players, supporters and owners. He is well-liked in the football world by those in the game and those who sit in the stands. What shone through was his passion for football. What also came across clearly is that Joe is the kind of natural leader who could be successful in almost any field due to his emotional intelligence, preparation and ability to galvanise a group of individuals behind a common cause.

Royle moved from Oldham to Everton and established himself with the supporters quickly. 'It was really important to do that. We were in a relegation fight and those players needed to give their all for the club. I described the players as 'Dogs of War'. The fans saw that in the way we played and they loved it. The way we played was all about passion and commitment, it had to be because we knew we couldn't compete with some teams in technical ability. Being 'Dogs of War' gave us an identity and a connection with what the fans wanted. You then get the fans understanding from Day 1 what your players will give and what their strengths are.'

The phrase prepared Everton's loyal supporters for a style of football that would be driven by a gritty determination. Royle chose this phrase specifically as he knew this approach would be the only one that could secure top-flight survival for Everton as they struggled in the relegation zone.

'The people that are important in making any plans you've got come to life are the vocal supporters who run the fanzines, the owners and, of course, the players,' he told us. 'It is imperative to understand the background of a club and the direction they wish to go.

'The first thing I look to do before I start at a club is to understand the history and the culture. That's what I make sure is in my messages, particularly in that week before Day 1 in the building. I engage with the supporters because they are the ones who own the culture. With the owners, you need to manage upward and at times you need to educate them. They need to be aware of the culture and they need to understand what you believe are realistic expectations.'

Royle was clear that when dealing with owners, or those above you in the organisational hierarchy, that there are no winners if it becomes an acrimonious relationship. 'You need to listen to the owner because at the end of the day it is their club. You also need to be fully aware that you both want the same thing. You need to work together or the job is much more difficult if that is not the case.

'You've got to use that week or month before a ball is

kicked to establish these relationships because it's much more difficult when the action starts. That said, you need to be really clear what success is so that you are both on the same page.'

Zones 1-4 – Managing your time

Once you have established the three P's, you can begin to look at a fourth 'P' – Priorities.

Micky and I both use Stephen Covey's 'Urgent/Important Matrix' which is a great tool for quickly defining what needs doing and when in four zones (see below).

It has a secondary purpose for allowing a manager or leader to gain an understanding of how they are spending their time.

Urgent/Important Matrix

	URGENT	NOT URGENT
IMPORTANT	I > Crises > Pressing problems > Firefighting > Major scrap & rework > Deadline-driven projects	II > Prevention > Production capability activities > Relationship building > Recognizing new opportunities > Planning > Re-creation
NOT IMPORTANT	III > Interruptions > Some Calls > Some Mail > Some Reports > Some Meetings > Proximate pressing matters > Popular activities > Some scrap & rework	IV > Trivia > Busywork > Some mail > Some phone calls > Time-wasters > Pleasant activities

Micky explains: 'Time management in the first 100 days is critical. Spend the wrong time on the wrong things and set a direction of travel which does not move the critical elements forward resulting in loss of focus and, whatever this looks like in your place of work, loss of the dressing room. It might be a loss of a staff room or a loss of a department, whatever the case may be, you've got to spend your time on the things that give you the best chance of winning.'

Sam Allardyce has needed to have immediate impact in several clubs that he has guided from relegation. 'Clearly, you need to deal with that which is urgent and important to begin with but you just can't forget about the non-urgent but important things. Like I said before, you'll get that reaction, you'll ride the crest of that wave but be sure that the wave won't last. You've got to get the most of the time you're on that wave but be ready for when the water goes from underneath you and you're now out at sea with only that long-term plan to guide you forward.

'The urgent matters when I've been at Crystal Palace or Sunderland are those that are usually highly visible and of immediate importance. At least, their importance is felt by others both internally and externally. At most of the clubs I've been into, they're shipping goals. If you're thinking about changing the style of play or trying to be more attractive, then you're in trouble because the urgent stuff needs fixing first.'

Ole Gunnar Solskjær moved skilfully into this important/ not urgent zone quickly during his first few weeks as manager of Manchester United. It was crucial to use the early 'honeymoon period' to make changes he saw as key to longer-term success. As with any early buy-in or winning runs that often come from a change in leadership, it will come to an end. So when it goes, the changes that can support longer-term success must be firmly in place.

It is easy to be drawn to the urgent non-important. Covey gives the examples of the distraction of a ringing phone which interrupts a key discussion. In football this ringing phone could be the pressures of supporters' online fanzines or media pressures. Keeping a balanced mind and operating in the top two zones is key. To fall into the fourth zone is simply irresponsible. Of course, this can happen, which is where a strong team of support is essential to keep the manager on track.

Zone 1 – Everton 2, Liverpool 0

'You've got to win. It's as simple as that,' says Micky. 'The fans will stick with you for a bit if you've got that build-up right but you've got to get a win early on. You've got to give them something they can grab onto and something they can believe in. That's why you've got to make sure you start at the right time with a club if possible. Whatever your matches are, whatever your judgement is, both small and large wins, you've got to win.'

The result of Joe Royle's preparation for Day 1 at Everton culminated in a 2-0 win over arch-rivals Liverpool in the 1994-1995 season. Royle, who had a midfield that consisted of Barry Horne, Joe Parkinson and John Ebbrell, had perfectly assessed the qualities and limitations. He had conjured up an image of warriors amongst the Everton faithful. He gave the players the best chance of winning that first game. It was that understanding of the three P's which allowed him to get his priorities right for his first training sessions and his first actions which were to address the culture and climate of the club.

Micky agreed wholeheartedly with this. 'All of this book is really about giving yourself the best chance of winning in football and leadership in those first 100 days. So it might sound glaringly obvious that you need to win early. It is so important, though, if you get early wins that you give yourself time for the medium and the long-term. That first win for me against Wrexham, in the local derby, was massive. It gave the fans the belief that I could turn this around. It wasn't that it was everything but it did give us that momentum early on.'

This zone incorporates crisis management and immediate problems which must be tackled by the manager. The manner in which they do this is what forms the initial impressions of players, supporters, those in the boardroom and the forensic media. You've also got to understand that in life, like football, you are often forced into Zone 1. So you've got to make sure that your principles are right and that you've been allowed to build up those winning principles over time because of your early wins.

Zone 2 – Heavy metal football

'I call these our principles,' Micky explains. 'We plan our core principles as a coaching staff. I'll give you an example, you don't leave the back four (defensive positions) unless you can affect the attacking play. It's really simple isn't it but when players do it, because they make mistakes and they're human, we bring them back to these principles. If you've not got principles then you'll just change game by game and sometimes minutes by minute, then no-one knows what to do and you're sunk! Any organisation has got to have principles and you've got to be able to communicate them, the reasons why we have them and then make sure you hold people to it.'

Ole Gunnar Solskjær talked about a similar approach. 'Our principles are power, pace and personality. It is what we talk about a lot. We like to change our system because we don't like the opposition to know how we play. I'll give you the example of Everton (with whom United had drawn 1-1 the weekend before we spoke). We knew how they were going to play, 4-4-2. So we set up to know who they play the ball out to. We turned the ball over and we scored. That is sticking to principles.

'It's important in the way that you recruit players because now when you are bringing new people into the club, you know what you are looking for because you've got principles. You won't end up with a lot of individual ingredients that don't add up to a meal.'

This is perhaps one of the biggest learning points for me as a school leader. What I came to realise in my build-up to Day 1 as a headteacher is that there were some routines across the school but there was a sense of a lack of clarity over many principles and processes. As a school we now have established principles: things like, 'warn, move and remove' when dealing with disruptive students. They also take the form of behaviours – being outside classrooms to greet students and reducing poor behaviour on corridors. Like any set of principles that play a part in culture, they are developing and still being embedded in our school.

There is more to Zone 2 than purely principles. A great deal of self-discipline, driven by fundamental beliefs and conviction, is required for managers to operate in Zone 2. Not to mention supreme leadership of those who are above, below and external of the club's hierarchy.

Zone 2 is vision and values based behaviours which are balanced and based on longer-term views. In a football context, they are redeveloping the habits of the team, ensuring the nutrition programme is effective, developing good relationships with the supporters and becoming a leader of the entire club.

The managers who achieve long-term success, which in football terms would be anything more than two seasons, personify the club's vision and mission. Take for example Jürgen Klopp who arrived at Liverpool and used the term 'heavy metal football'.

This was a metaphor which the supporters latched onto and could immediately relate to. It was not the vision of the past, although respectful of years gone by, but an exciting future. It was Zone 2 thinking in that it was not an urgent matter, to galvanise the imagination of the Liverpool supporters, but it was essential to set out what could be possible. Suddenly, Liverpool had a modern identity which was being personified by their colourful, charismatic leader who captivated the crowd like a rock star on the stage at Glastonbury.

Zone 3 - The enemy of progress

As much as a resolve is required to focus on the first two Zones, the pressure to bask in Zone 3 should not be ignored. In football, the distractions are frequent and relentless. Whether it's the pressure to respond to incessant media speculation or the intense, emotive calls from supporters' groups, distractions are constant. The enemy of short, medium and long-term decisions that will move the team forward, is Zone 3. Key questions can identify when urgent matters are non-important and simply noise:

1. Is the matter essential to the vision of the manager or leader?

2. Will the matter enhance the performance of the players or key personnel?

3. Could the matter cause significant damage to the performance of the team?

4. Could the matter damage the established important relationships?

If the answer to all of the above is 'no', then the issue clearly belongs in Zone 3 and worthy of, possibly, acknowledgement rather than any action that detracts from those in Zone 1 and 2.

Zone 4 – The comfort zone

Consistent work in this area is most often caused when it relates to an area of the job which feels most comfortable for the manager. Operating in this area and in Zone 3, on a regular basis, will lead to failure.

And now the day comes – believe in yourself

After a successful appointment and the three P's of preparation, the day ultimately arrives when the manager sits in the dugout, the headteacher stands in front of the school and the CEO addresses his colleagues. Micky and the voices of world-famous managers rang in my ears the night before my first day as a headteacher. I called Micky for advice the night before my new beginning. His advice, as ever, was clear and consistent: 'Believe in yourself, do what you think is the right thing to do, smile and have confidence that you understand the task ahead.'

I thought back to the words of Joe Royle: 'Never underestimate the value of a smile.' Like Ole, Joe, Sam and Micky, I'd done my homework on this school and the people who made up its community. I believed I understood what was required to channel the potential, tackle the obstacles and help the school build upon the successes of the past. That said, like many leaders in my position, I went to bed with a knot in my stomach and the usual self-doubts that as humans can either fuel positive energies or cripple a person with uncertainty. The following 100 days will reveal what effect this energy would have on me.

Reflections

1. Why do you believe you were chosen for the job?

2. How will this impact upon your behaviours and approach to your first 100 days?

3. What is your end point? Where are you now? How will you bridge the gap?

4. What are the obstacles you will need to overcome?

5. What deliberate steps will you take to connect with your team and stakeholders?

6. How will you collect the views of the people who form the opinions of others?

7. Where do the required actions sit in the urgent/important matrix?

8. How does this classification affect the strategic plan for the first 100 days and beyond?

9. Are the current staff capable of meeting the demands of the negotiated success?

10. What will your action mapper look like before Day 1 and how will you allow time to reflect on this as the first 100 days evolve?

Chapter Three

DAY 1

 Writing your story

Create a script with a happy ending

A vision is a story. It's a bestselling novel. It's a blockbuster movie. It's a narrative that connects people and encourages them to want to be a part of it. The best visions are clear. They give an exciting picture of the future. They are the destination on a route map which may never quite be reached but set a course for excitement, engagement and energy.

When the direction is set, those following the vision must work toward that goal cohesively. Like any movie or novel, visions need a script. They need actors that will play key roles in order to make the story come to life. These four steps are the fundamentals to kicking off your first 100 days:

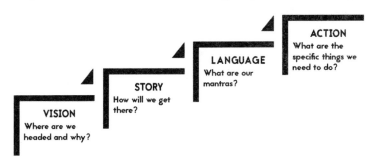

1: Vision – the class of '66

Leaders in football need to be clear about their story from the beginning. When he took over as England manager, Kevin Keegan was specific in his ambition: 'We want to try and match what the '66 team did. They had a bit of luck and we will need that too.' Winning the World Cup was the ultimate objective and told fans, press and players that Keegan was aiming for the biggest prize of all.

'A vision epitomises the beliefs that the manager has about the possibility for the future,' says Micky. 'They must be related to the negotiated success described earlier while not being overly pragmatic. They must give purpose, offer a cause and allow one to visualise what the future will look like under this new leadership regime.

'In the world of football, a vision can be a style of play, a social identity or a global brand. For the manager, this must be translated in an objective. In the short-term it is quite simply to win. The medium to long-term objectives that are the foundation of the vision can be promotion, avoiding relegation or winning the Champions League. At Tranmere, we needed to tap into what was special about this club, this area and these people. Whatever company or school you're in, you'll have that unique thing that makes your organisation distinct from any other.'

When Carlo Ancelotti signed in as manager of Everton Football Club in 2019, he did exactly the same. When asked why he had agreed to join the Blues just days after leaving Napoli, he responded: 'The ambition of the club, the history that this club has, the tradition, the atmosphere of the supporters…' At once Evertonians knew that Ancelotti understood their club.

Micky continued: 'I know from the fans I spoke to that talking up the area and these people was something that hadn't happened for a long time. It was my mantra, we are Tranmere and we represent the hard-working people of Birkenhead properly. That kind of a vision is not a glamorous one but it's a vision that will resonate with the people it needs to. You only hit the spot with a vision if you truly understand the people and the place. It gave us our core purpose.' This is a message Micky has since taken to Dundee United as he talks of the history, the legends and the Silvery Tay.

It is a mantra plucked from the handbook of a man who created a famous football dynasty just a few miles from Prenton Park – Liverpool messiah Bill Shankly. Time and time again, Shankly would remind his players that their job was to represent the people of Liverpool when they pulled on the red shirt. As more than 100,000 fans turned up en masse in the city centre to greet the team after they had lost the 1971 FA Cup final, Shankly told them: 'Since I came here to Liverpool, and to Anfield, I have drummed it into our players time and again that they are privileged to play for you. And if they didn't believe me, they believe me now.'

Micky spoke to me as we walked toward an Argentinian steak house in the heart of Liverpool city centre. He spoke to me passionately about the importance of that first day so much. I was approaching my first day as a headteacher in my own right and so I listened intently.

As I drove to school, I had butterflies in my stomach that fluttered with a touch of self-doubt and feelings that I have come to know as 'imposter syndrome'. Imposter syndrome is a psychological term and I believe it is something you can plan for.

I am not worthy

Leaders can become overwhelmed by the enormity of the task. It is easy for the mind to slip into the zone of worst case scenario and a mode of self-preservation from the fear of an unknown future. The work to tackle the VUCA world is certainly powerful here. Understanding the syndrome can also help. My personal experience of imposter syndrome is an inclination to remember unkind words that have been said to me in my professional life or childhood. I can't explain how I do it but I try to accept these memories and use them an inspiration rather than a negative. I visualise the success I believe can be achieved and at this point I used the visualisation of my family, who I knew would be proud of me in this new role. In particular, I thought of my grandmother who passed away the previous year. She always had such personal strength and a belief that I could achieve whatever I set my mind to. As I addressed the staff and the students, I can't explain enough how I felt her presence in that room.

On that first day, I gave a presentation that was a narrative. It was a narrative that used the analogy of a voyage. The voyage was a nautical one that clearly defined where we were headed, why we could achieve this, what we needed to do to get there and when we would know if we had been successful. I captured this voyage with a vision statement that stated our desire '...to become a world class school that encourages our students to want to make the world a better place.' It was deliberately bold and deliberately not linked to an Ofsted grading, the definition of which can change regularly. I explained it to the whole staff first, that included everyone in the kitchen, administration, site team, IT support, teaching and support staff. This needed to be our vision and it was borne from a statement from one colleague who said in conversation: 'It might be good enough for other schools but it's not good enough for here because this is St Bede's.'

#2 – United's story – Fergie time again

From the first one of his first 100 days, Ole Gunnar Solskjær realigned players and staff across the club back to the traditions and historic culture of the club that had won so much under Sir Alex Ferguson.

'On our first day, I signed contracts at 8.45am. We'd only found out the day before because Mourinho had been sacked. I came in the building and it was smiles everywhere. People were really happy to see us. I felt really welcomed back and it was really like coming home. Then about 11am, I got the players together. We spoke to them about what an honour it was to be at Manchester United. I said I had been following them on the telly and it was a privilege to be working with players like this.

'We talked about high expectations, having some fun and

even surprising a few people. 'Let's enjoy one day at a time and start winning again.' Later that day, I remember walking out and hearing people saying, 'Finally, we're talking about being Manchester United again.'

'We wanted to project to the players that we've been on one of the greatest journeys ever with Sir Alex Ferguson and now we want to do that again,' explained Mick Phelan. This was the story. Mick and Ole were beginning a narrative with the players and they were setting out what type of characters they would need in this blockbuster. There would be those for who this story was not applicable. They likely sat there and questioned what their role would be. However, what was important was that this vision was now being translated into a story which would tell the tale of how they would reach their happy ending from the opening credits which began on Day 1.

Solsjkaer and Mick Phelan had begun to start a process of turnaround and realignment. In terms of motivation, he had brought back a sense of purpose, belonging and tradition.

'After we had spoken to the players, there were lots of media interviews. That was followed by a meeting between me, Mick and Jimmy for about one hour. I was lucky because that night was the staff do. I went along, gave a speech and had a bit of a dance.'

I asked Ole whether this was something that was the norm for United managers. 'No, I don't think so,' he replied. 'When I first got the job I called Sir Alex and he said I was ready but to make sure I looked after the staff at Carrington. (Ryan) Giggsy texted me as well to say congratulations and he said the same: 'Look after the staff at Carrington. We are a family at United and they know that.'

Mick Phelan added: 'I've always said this, the team behind the team is massive. At a club like this, everyone has to feel like they have something to contribute. We wanted everyone to have a voice. Now people do their jobs in their departments but they know our door is open and they can come and share their ideas.'

Green Bay Packers – know the end to the story

Legendary American Football coach Vince Lombardi is one of the most revered sporting leaders of all time and he had a clear vision and was relentless in his pursuit of this vision. In his own words: 'The difference [between a good coach and an average coach] is knowing what you want, and knowing what the end is supposed to look like. If a coach doesn't know what the end is supposed to look like, he won't know it when he sees it.'

The end, for Lombardi, was a vision of a successful Green Bay Packers team that won six NFL Championships and then two Super Bowls. He achieved this repeatedly due to his ability to link goals to vision, change with the competitive environment, resist the temptation to be swayed by minor setbacks and remain focused on a vision of success. Like Solskjær, he understood what was required to win. He saw the behaviours, attitudes and routines that were required.

Like other great leaders, Lombardi believed the key to the vision was the 'why' rather than the 'how'. In the book detailing his principles 'The Lombardi Rules', the author, who is also his son, quotes his father as saying: 'I never tell a player, 'this is my way, now do it'… instead, I say, 'this is how we do it, and this is why we do it.' This notion of leading with 'why' links directly to the premise of Simon Sinek's concept of 'start with why' referred to earlier. Sinek describes the 'Golden Circle' and cites that all highly effective leaders start from inside out – with 'why', then 'how' and finally 'what'. Sinek is clear that, in opposition to this approach, 'when most organisations or people think, act or communicate, they do so from the inside out.'

Like Lombardi and Micky, Ole Gunnar Solskjær talked to his players, board and fans in a manner which showed he understood the industrial, hard-working 'why' of United that leads to the glory. It was not about styles of play, it was not about the egos of players or the manager, it was all about this club and what it meant to so many people in Manchester and around the world. As mentioned earlier, Ole's message was so authentic and fluent, he inspired the whole team and support staff to begin talking about what it meant to be part of Manchester United. The whole organisation could begin to become realigned with a 'why' linked to the great traditions and past glories.

Simon Sinek states that major companies such as Apple, Southwest Airlines or leaders such as Martin Luther King operate from 'why' and then work outward. Sinek highlights that we are drawn to 'why' people do what they do rather than 'how' or 'what' they do as this taps into the limbic brain. Sinek affirms that people do not buy or believe in what people do but rather why they do it. This reflected the drivers in the limbic brain which is responsible for our feelings such as trust and loyalty. The 'how' and the 'what' are housed in our neo-cortex which is responsible for logic and language. In other words, we feel before we can articulate. People often refer to such emotional responses as 'gut instinct' however this response to a compelling vision is biological and developed in our limbic brain.

The Golden Circle and the Limbic System

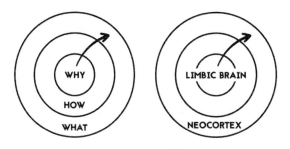

All at Harvard University follow a vision to '...develop leaders who will one day make a global difference'. At the world famous motorbike company, Harley Davidson, the vision is, 'to fulfil dreams through the experiences of motor-cycling'. Disney holds the wholesome vision to 'make people happy' while Arsenal Football Club pledges togetherness as the route to success – Victoria Concordia Crescit (Victory Through Harmony).

All of the aforementioned garner a sense of 'why' and attractive emotional rather than logical responses. They all seek to feed what Dr Steve Peters famously refers to as the chimp in our brain.

In turnaround situations visions can be quite different. Sam Allardyce, when taking over a struggling Premier League side, does not share visions based on philosophical grounds or notions of attractive styles of play for the viewing thousands. Rather, Allardyce will talk about basics and principles required to get the job done.

Allardyce talks in points, percentages, principles and pragmatism. This approach is consistent amongst leaders who take over situations that require a turnaround in a short space of time. In 1993, when IBM was in trouble and Lou Gerstner was handed the responsibility of CEO, he famously said, "The last thing IBM needs right now is a vision." Gerstner recognised that it was pragmatism rather than an ethereal vision that was required to make the rapid change required to save the company.

Tuesday Humby, who we met earlier, was nominated for the Global Teacher of the Year award and has been given many educational accolades. She explained how she also did not begin with a wordy vision but rather a systematic, stepped approach to a turnaround which could save the school.

In all three cases, there is a vision but the vision is one driven by the need for survival which dominates the inner-chimp. In the first 100 days, the leader must arrive at a vision quickly that recognises the necessity of the situation.

Once the vision is shared, a narrative is written and spoken which details the story of the vision. What sort of story it will be, what the ending will be and how we will all get there, is up to the characters involved. It is the job of the leader to explain what the vision or desired ending will be, describe what the story will be leading up to this ending and they must share who the key characters will be.

For Solsjkaer, behaving in this manner is really just an extension of a humble and empathetic persona. However, it immediately lifted the whole atmosphere at the club as now they had 'one of their own' in charge and they were desperate for him to do well.

By visiting the staff party on his first day, when he could have been sat at home analysing game footage, Ole got his 100 days off to a good start by building his team, not just the playing staff but the entire club, around him. The momentum had shifted drastically in 24 hours and, in 48 hours, that momentum would be there for all to see in Ole's first match in charge.

#3: Language – Sean Dyche's sticky words

It is imperative that the vision matches the situation. We sat with Burnley manager Sean Dyche in his office at the Burnley training ground. We arranged to chat for 45 minutes but the conversation continued for three hours as we were all engrossed in the subject matter.

I had always imagined that the offices of Premier League managers would be grand rooms with pictures of past glories. However, this room was functional and clinical but had everything necessary for meetings and one to one discussions.

Dyche is a relaxed and confident character who has mastered the art of, as he describes, 'sticky words'.

As he sat in his training shirt, shorts and white trainers, he opened up to us about the methods he has used to create a culture at Burnley which has seen them gain promotion to the Premier League and now become a team and a club that can punch well above its weight.

Dyche got his vision across quickly on Day 1 at his press conference in 2012 and then in a meeting with the players. He explained to Micky and I: 'When I interviewed at the club I told the board that I felt the relationship between the fans and the club was strained. I presented a PowerPoint to the interviewers that had a bit about my playing career and then more about the position I felt Burnley was currently in. My view of where Burnley was at was that they were mis-aligned, the fans thought they should be top of the league after coming out of the Premier League two years previous.

'They'd spent quite a lot of money coming out of the Premier League. I described that I felt the connection between the town, the club and the people was at a bit of a stretch. I thought the commonality of the club was the underdog fighting but now people were just saying, 'why aren't we top of the league?' It was delusional in its truth.

'My perception of Burnley was everyone in it together, punching above their weight. In my interview and with the players, I talked about 'legs, hearts and minds'. You'll see it all over the training ground now and that was from my interview. Where that came from was legs – you need to be able to run; hearts – from Brian Clough, who always said to me, even as a kid, if you haven't got hearts on the team bus then you're in trouble. And minds came from Arsène

Wenger who said you have the ground floor for physical, the second floor for technical and the third floor is your roof. If you haven't got a roof then…well you need a roof!'

Dyche's vision fitted with the values and essence of the town. He was not a popular choice, as he was acutely aware. 'I had my friends all over social media and they were telling me just how unpopular I was as a choice. I knew I was going for a job that the people didn't want me to get! There were other favourites they wanted. In my first press conference I tried to get across what I'd deliver. I told the fans that I couldn't guarantee winning every week but I could guarantee them sweat on the shirt. Sticky words. They knew what I meant and I knew I could deliver that.'

The result of the 'legs, hearts and minds' mantra and the 'sweat on the shirt' promise, was that Sean Dyche has aligned his vision for the club with the values of the hard working people of Burnley. They again saw their club as the plucky underdog and, over time, the values of the town have become the values of the team.

This is not a process that ended after Day 1 as Dyche explained: 'I still use words like 'relentless', we're relentless in everything we do. We go for 95 minutes not 90 minutes. We will out-run anyone. We're the fittest team in the league. Go hard or go home. We use all of those words in our com-munications with the players, the fans and the media. It creates a culture and precedent. I knew we had reached that tipping point with the players when one lad was belting down the tunnel for the warm-up. I heard an opposition player laugh a bit and say, 'What do you lot do that for?

Sprint down the tunnel and all that.' Our player, who wasn't necessarily the first person you'd expect to buy into this just said: 'Because it's what we do.' Then you know you've got them and they get it. Your vision just became what they do.'

A spontaneous phone call to Sir Alex

Sir Alex Ferguson inspired Dyche in a way that gave Burnley a mental edge that supported their eventual promotion to the Premier League. 'It was one of those funny things in life. I was walking in the park with my wife. I just told her I was going to give him a call,' he explained.

Dyche called Sir Alex asking for advice on how to keep the team focused on their target of promotion and calm under the increasing media interest in their progress. He explained the advice he received: 'He told me to keep it simple, he told me that he'd seen how hard my team were running. Then he said, 'You know my team could run? You know how we out-ran other teams and how we always grabbed late goals because we were so fit in the second half of the season?' Dyche acknowledged all of the aforementioned as understood and widely known across the world of football. 'You know why we were able to do that?' Sir Alex asked. 'Because I told everyone that we were fitter, stronger and better in the second half of the season. That's why.'

A commonly held 'fact' in Premier League history became so because Sir Alex Ferguson persuaded everyone it was a truth, most importantly his own players, the supporters and the opposing teams. 'We didn't do anything different in the second half of the season,' Sir Alex went on.

Dyche continued: 'You also hear the lads using your language around the training ground. Tripps (Kieran Trippier, former Burnley player and now England regular and plying his trade at Atlético Madrid) was a classic for it. Tripps would be shouting out 'it's a fair one, gaffer' or 'we're all online, gaffer' during our sessions. Some of the coaching staff asked me what I thought about them buzzing off my phrases because those are lines I use a lot. I would say that it's great because they might be having a bit of a laugh but you know your messages are getting through.'

Both Micky and Sean Dyche listen very carefully to their key messages or buzz words being used. Micky added: 'I've been telling the lads that they need to suffer and be prepared to suffer more than the opposition. I can hear that getting through now because they're shouting that at each other before they head out for a game.' The message from these top managers was clear: use simple and punchy words and phrases to get your message and principles across. Then listen for those words being used by the team or the coaching staff. This quiet observation of shifting culture can signal small wins for the leader and give an assurance that the key instructions are being heard and understood.

But as Dyche said to Micky and I: 'It's not as easy as it sounds in the management books.' There are many examples of football managers who mis-matched vision with the requirements of the job. Frank de Boer lasted 77 days as manager of Crystal Palace, losing his four games in a row in a fashion that prompted the Palace board the take action. Football pundit Jermaine Jenas put this down to a mistaken approach to change the ethos of the club. Speaking on BBC 5 Live, Jenas explained: 'It's Crystal Palace, you do what you're good at. You get the place absolutely rocking. This whole 'let's change our ethos', and do what? Become Ajax and pop the ball about and play triangles all over the place? That is not what you're ever going to be.'

Visions must match the culture and the situation which can be established by following the steps detailed in the opening chapters. The vision must be clear and attainable as well as engaging. And it must also be part of the negotiated success discussions held with the owner prior to the opening day.

The owner or CEO must be clear that, should there be a shift in ethos or approach that will impact culture, this will take time and may not be met with immediate success. In the case of de Boer or other high-profile early departures, the negotiated success could well have been at the root cause of the problem.

John C. Maxwell explains in his book 'Leadershift' that leaders effectively sell their stories by an underpinning authenticity.

This authenticity provides the answer to three key questions that members of a team will ask of their leader.

1. Do you care about me? Those who look to the football manager will question the intentions of their leader. They will be asking themselves whether this individual has the desire to improve them as individuals. It is aligned with the thoughts of Brendan Rodgers who, as quoted in Mike Carson's League Managers

Association (LMA)-supported book, 'The Manager', believes all players walk around with a metaphorical message on their forehead. The message reads 'make me feel important'. Players only buy into the story their manager wishes to create if they feel important and they see the role that is there for them.

2. Can I trust you? Honesty and integrity are crucial in developing a sense that leaders can be believed. The vision, words and intentions of the manager must be a lived reality every day. When integrity is questioned through erratic behaviours or a lack of consistency, then trust can be broken. Trust gives players a sense of safety and security that leads to a buy-in to the leader which offers a depth of commitment.

3. Will you help me? This last question comes down to professionalism and competency. These two qualities are crucial in establishing sustained leadership and deliver on the story explained at the beginning of the first 100 days. Such help is delivered through the leader developing the group and the individuals every day. As Micky explains: 'We have to remember why we are leaders. We are there to make a group of individuals better, collectively and so that the football club is in a better place than when we've landed there.' This is perhaps why Micky attracts players to his teams as they know he cares, they can trust him and he will improve them. No doubt Jürgen Klopp is the same.

It is important to remember that great visions and inspiring messages are just that. They need to be quickly followed up on the training ground, in staff training sessions, amendments to internal processes and any other functional way which has a positive impact. What a successful Day 1 does give a leader, in any walk of life, is momentum to do some heavy lifting in those first 100 days which allow for 'quick wins' that develop confidence in the leader.

#4: Action – the axeman cometh (or does he?)

When Mark Palios walked toward the offices of the Football Association in London, he was only too aware of the media perceptions and portrayal of his methodology in the business world. As Micky and I sat in his office, Palios sipping a cup of black coffee, sat forward in his chair and recounted Day 1 at The FA. 'When I went into The FA, I thought I understood what I needed to do but I didn't really. The press had already billed it as the axe-man cometh. Everyone's pre-conceived idea is that an insolvency man comes in and cuts people. When I first met the staff, I simply said to them to keep doing what they were doing until I told them to stop. I also pulled out some of the things I knew they were doing well and praised them for that, such as grassroots work.' For Palios, this alleviated the pressure of making snap judgements without fully understanding the context of The FA and it also allowed him to fully understand what his priorities were.

As he sat back in his chair, he reiterated the point of avoiding falling into the trap of taking actions without understanding the complexities of any organisation and submitting to the 'something must be done brigade'. As he paused for thought, he looked at Micky and I saying: 'I came in the August (2003) and by early September you've got the fight at Old Trafford, eight on a charge (following a high-profile spat between players of Manchester United and Arsenal resulting from a missed last-minute penalty). By the end of September, Rio Ferdinand missed a drug test and I've got the threat of the first England players strike on my hands. You'd say that's a pretty full agenda, but there was more. I needed £27 million in 21 days, otherwise, Wembley would crater. I persuaded the bank to give us an overdraft for the first time in The FA's history.

'We'd also changed the disciplinary process for the entire history of The FA. I knew I needed to reform that process. We also had Euro 2004 coming up and UEFA were at odds with us if there was any repeat of the fan violence. I actually had a completely different set of priorities to the ones the press believed I had. So, you've actually got to be very strong on what your priorities are.'

What intrigued Micky and I was the patience and calmness that Palios entered the situation with. It would have been easy at The FA to tackle the high-profile priorities first and perhaps appease the press in dealing with the stories that were most prominent in the news. All companies, teams and schools have external pressures which can drive a leader to take their eye off the key priorities which, as Palios skillfully articulated, can only be understood after time is taken to get to grips with the internal workings of an organisation.

Palios explained why gaining knowledge before acting was so pivotal: 'The thing that you're fighting for in the first 100 days of a turnaround is the credibility of the management team and the organisation (internally and externally). As my priority at The FA, what I had to do was rebuild the credibility. The issues with that were the disciplinary system was hurting us, we were bust, so how could we tell the Premier League what we needed them to do?

'I called all of my team together at The FA in the first week. I said that this was the best story never told about the 40,000 clubs and all of the work at grassroots. There is a balance to change in the first 100 days.

'I told everyone at The FA that I liked a lot of what they were doing. I upped the morale by telling them there was a lot of good work going on. You've got to give yourself time in those first 100 days. I defy anyone to know their priorities before they go in.'

While small wins can be attained quickly, and good impressions can be made instantaneously, it is very clear from the vast experience of Mark Palios, the leaders in their first 100 days should seek first to understand before they are understood.

Leaders should set priorities only when they are acutely aware of three points: people, time and money, which Palios describes as his 'Turnaround Triangle'.

Writing the script for the season ahead

While Mark Palios describes a clear 'Turnaround Triangle', Sam Allardyce has a similarly pragmatic approach to make changes that his players and staff understand. These actions come in the form of a script-like narrative that he draws up with his teams. The development of such a script is akin to the strategies of renowned psychotherapist Claude Steiner. Both Allardyce and Claude Steiner advocate an approach which shows the desired ending and then works back to help individuals really think about what is required to achieve that goal.

When Allardyce sits his new side down, either at the beginning of the season or when he has taken over, he asks them to write their script for the season. In conversation with Micky, Big Sam explained: 'The days of planning for a year, two years, five years are gone now, especially in the Premier League. Your vision now is for the next month.'

Allardyce asks the players to decide where they believe they can finish. He then analyses the data of previous seasons and assesses how many points will be required in order to achieve that goal. The players then look at the fixtures and decide where the points are coming from. They set their script for the season.

This script is broken down into five sections, which include eight games at a time with six games in the final section. Allardyce explains: 'You need to understand the importance of the first eight games. I remember, as a player, you'd think a loss in game one or two was not that important because there was loads of the season left. I need the players to understand that these games are all vitally important if I'm to achieve the success I've negotiated with the owners.'

Allardyce goes into greater detail with his players and staff by using equations generated from statistical analysis of the Premier League. He shares with the playing staff various calculations such as; *number of X goals scored v X number of goals conceded = league position X or number of X set pieces scored v X number conceded = X games won.* This session allows the players to gain an understanding of the relative importance for each aspect of training and during games. This also serves as a driver in offering a belief that if they can reduce the number of goals conceded overall or become more effective from set-pieces then the opportunity to exceed expectations is a reality. A script is created with the ending becoming adaptable based on the performance of the team and the individuals within it.

Once the script is written the behaviours required to achieve this narrative or script are discussed. Each week the players are reminded what is required in order to achieve the ending to the story, or season, that they desire. This has implications on training, team selection, mentality of the players, awareness of the targets for each game. When the players come off script, for example losing to a team just above or below them in the table, the challenge is then to take points off the top teams to compensate for this. In Allardyce's changing room, the story of the season is told before it begins with the ending clear. The players then know what is required to make this story or vision become a reality.

Claude Steiner was a French-born American psychotherapist and writer who wrote extensively about transactional analysis and focused specifically on life scripts among other concepts. The premise for the individual is that we have a subconscious belief of how our lives will pan out. Often, the teams inherited by Sam Allardyce had stories that ended in relegation should they not be addressed emphatically from Day 1. Allardyce, by defining the requirements of success and negotiating a points tally, is giving the narrative of the vision which breaks down the over-arching mission into pragmatic objectives and actions. He is offering an alternative script that can be followed by a change of approach and attitude.

Tuesday Humby took a similar approach in the construction of a narrative which would act as a script for the students, staff and parents of her school. Tuesday shared with staff key milestones that were effectively SMART goals. They detailed the small steps that would be taken, the matches that could be won, over a set period of time. The result of achieving these gains were illustrated in the same way that the consequence of achieving a certain number of wins has on a football team's season. Tuesday marked and celebrated each time a milestone was reached.

She explained to me: 'It was a great visual. I was surprised how much it gave confidence to our staff especially when we met our short-term goals. They grew in confidence. It was a simple presentation of bubbles. Each bubble represented a goal. When we met that goal, like passing our academy inspection, I lit up the bubble and shared it with the staff. It meant that we were all part of achieving the success we craved and then we knew what the next step was.' This simple but effective presentation was the signposting tool which helped the previously beleaguered staff see that they were winning. As they grew in confidence, the scripts of the individuals at the school changed from one that propagated behaviour akin to characters in a disaster movie to one which would become the glorious victory over adversity.

Steiner explores the origin of human behaviours which is often the process of a leading manager. From Day 1, the manager must observe the behaviours of the players and decide that which will facilitate the success of the goal and that which will become an obstacle. This will, of course, be developed over time but Day 1 is the moment to set vision and alert players and staff of the expectations for all which must be adhered to. Both Sam Allardyce and Tuesday Humby give clear routes of success that are transparent and incremental. As a result, members of the team are furnished with hope and a sense of the possibility of victory from the start. That hope is created from a vision with the sense of possibility being grounded in the script.

My first day at school

When I first walked into the building at St Bede's, months before Day 1 in the hotseat, it was clear that this was a tight community. Many of the staff had been there for over a decade and the staffroom was held together by a complex network of team and interpersonal dynamics. It was a staffroom that had seen a good amount of recent success and there was a confidence amongst individuals that was clear from the early conversations at an informal level.

Before I officially started in my role at the school, I needed to get under the skin of these dynamics to get an appreciation of the internal culture so that I could plan a way forward with my new community. By gaining an understanding of the organisational culture, I could then start to reduce any unpredictable volatilities of the new leadership role. I quickly realised that this would be crucial if I was to be successful in taking this school into their next imminent inspection by Ofsted, the external body that reviews all English state schools.

In addition to the questionnaire referred to earlier, I arranged meetings with the senior and middle leaders across the school. I asked them about their roles. We spoke about what they felt were the strengths and weaknesses of the school. What was fascinating about these meetings was the willingness of staff to open up about where they felt the school needed to be better. It became apparent that this was not a school that was beset by complacency but rather it was one which could be in danger of being riddled with professional frustrations.

As I built from Day 1, I pondered how I could get a collective impression of the school. Micky and I met up in a busy Italian restaurant in Liverpool to discuss our project. Micky suggested that we work on this concept of the first 100 days. Getting the knowledge of the challenge was key. 'Ask them what they think,' Micky said. 'They'll tell you. Speak to everyone. Ask the staff, the kids, the parents and the local shopkeeper. Get an understanding of what people think now because once it becomes your school and your ideas, they might not be so open with you.'

Over the course of the first few days, I asked as many people as possible in formal meetings, corridor chats, at the school gates and any other method I could find. The feedback I got helped me to empathise with people at every level of the school. It helped me contextualise the decisions I would have to make and the reactions I might get. I asked the previous head; he gave me a profile of every member of staff and all the history between the members of that team.

When dealing with any new group in this way, you must know the people and the culture, a bit of the history so you understand why some people are close and others don't speak to each other. When you are planning any change you reduce that VUCA world you are walking into, not entirely but significantly. Micky is a master of this. Employing the same approach regardless of the situation is a recipe for disaster and so many managers give great examples of taking a successful approach in one setting to their next club without the same result. This is something Micky has recognised and employed after taking up his new role at Dundee United.

As it was, when I got an understanding of St Bede's, I saw the staffroom and the school yard in a very different light. I saw the people in the staffroom as individuals. I saw who wanted promotion, who was frustrated, who was the trend-setter and who was the potential blocker to my leadership. Armed with that knowledge, I treated people as individuals. As I developed a better picture of the operational developments that were needed, I then worked with all the members of the team to find solutions that were of mutual benefit.

A winning start?

On my drive home after that first day, my car phone rang and Micky called to check in. We talked through the day. The day itself had been a success. There was a sense of anticipation in the school and an energy amongst our team.

I described the vision I shared through my presentation and the responses of the teachers. A few staff shared their excitement for a fresh start, others spoke to me in order to dig deeper about their role in this journey while others were clearly reserving judgement. Throughout the day, I had been following Micky's advice and speaking to my team about where they fitted in with this whole school plan. What I would stress to Micky, and to you reading this, is that the first day was the tip of the iceberg. The evaluation of the place, the people and the position allowed me to construct a vision and a set of values that matched the school. Just as Micky had described his winning start at Tranmere, so I believed I had started with a win at St Bede's.

However, Micky was quick to bring me back down to earth. 'You've done okay for Day 1 but don't forget, you've won nothing yet. You don't win anything in August in football and you haven't won anything in September in a school. Your matches start tomorrow and you've got to get some quick wins.' Of course, he was right.

'You've shared your plan, now where are you going to get your quick wins from?' Micky asked as he pressed me to see if I had thought beyond that first day. I had a plan but as Mike Tyson famously said: 'Everyone has a plan before they're punched in the face.' The rapid, unrelenting pace of headship was about to hit me like that punch in the face but I knew in spite of this, these quick wins would make or break my first month as a headteacher.

Reflections

1. What is your vision for the future of the team?

2. How will the story be told to describe the journey of the team in reaching this vision?

3. What language will you use to ensure everyone hears the same message?

4. What will your immediate actions be to show your intent to reach this vision?

5. How will you reach the limbic through a compelling 'why'?

6. If your leadership story was a film, what type of film is it?

7. Who are the characters?

8. What is the ending likely to be?

9. If this is not your desired ending, which characters need to be removed?

10. Who are the key characters you need to star in order for your script to be a blockbuster?

Chapter Four

THE FIRST 7 DAYS

 Quick wins

'Pick your team and sleep well'

After a packed first day which culminated in Ole Gunnar Solskjær visiting the staff Christmas party, Day 2 would be no less intense for one of the highest profile managerial roles in the football world. On 21st December, 2018, United travelled to their team hotel near Cardiff in preparation for their first game under the stewardship of Solskjær. The first day had been a roaring success and the love for Ole around the club was tangible. The question was, how would that translate to the players' performance on the pitch?

'I got a text from the manager (Sir Alex) who said: 'Pick your team and sleep well.' I sent him the players I was picking and I just got a message back: 'That'll do the job.' It was incredible to see the smile on both Ole and Mick's faces as that story was retold. They both held the tradition and culture of United in the highest of regards and those aspects are personified by the club's most successful manager and mentor to both, Sir Alex. They speak of him like a father. A father who was happy to be a support only when called upon but always there for them to ask for advice. It has clearly given Ole confidence and showed another important lesson for the first few days of the 100. Despite his position, he was not afraid to ask someone who had been there before. Ole was humble yet confident. He did not feel that asking someone else for their opinion was a weakness. Ole's leadership is authentic and that style includes a beautiful vulnerability that is rooted in an awareness that no one has all the answers.

The very next day, it took only three minutes for a new-look United to race into a 1-0 lead. 'Marcus crashed that free-kick home in three minutes and the whole thing felt like it had changed,' said Ole. 'We just went 4-3-3 and told the players to be free and express themselves.' Eventually, United would run out 5-1 winners away from home. It was a sensational start that showed a belief from the players and a joy that their new manager had a faith in them and a love for the club that they could now represent as a team.

The ovation from the crowd showed that United's huge away following emphatically approved of their new manager. He had shown from Day 1 that he was one of them and he stood for what they believed in. Early on the 23rd December, the day after the big win at Cardiff, Ole received the ultimate accolade via a text message. 'I've been out all night celebrating getting my club back.' The sender? Solskjær's mentor, father in football and United legend, Sir Alex Ferguson.

Such was the manner of the victory, the response from the players, fans and staff, the future looked bright for Ole's temporary tenure as United boss. This was the reaction the club had wanted but even they could not have predicted the sensational start that Solskjær and Phelan would make. The energy created by 'making people smile again' was palpable at Manchester United. Something was happening, it was not something in terms of football tactics or clever words, it was something deep and cultural. It was a re-awakening, a rebirth of a football club which had seemed almost moribund just a few days before. It was like old flames rekindling a love affair from many years before. The question now, would this renewed love affair continue or would it fizzle out in the morning? United fans and the world of football would not need to wait long to find out.

First dates – set the tone for a happy marriage

In one of our first conversations about this book, we sat with Tranmere's fitness coach, Andy Hodgen, and football development manager, Michael Kinsella, enjoying a glass of red wine and a great meal in a Liverpool fish restaurant. Micky joked about the romantic setting and with his typically insightful way, saw an analogy between a romantic date and your first 100 days as a leader of an organisation.

'When you're arriving at a new football club it is just like starting a relationship. You meet someone that you like. You make a connection. Then, if you like each other, you might start seeing each other more regularly. At some point it's going well so you emotionally invest and commit yourself.

With your new club, team or organisation, you basically start to care about what they think and what they say.

'Over time, a relationship can turn sour and you can get fed up of each other. In football, this might be losing matches or not playing the way the fans expect you to play. Alternatively, you might be doing really well and that can lead to a break in the relationship. Eventually, you both, or one of you, can want a change and so the relationship or your time as manager comes to an end. For some, like Sir Alex Ferguson or Arsène Wenger, you get married but most of the time in football, it's just a fling!'

Despite the precarious nature of football management, and most relationships, to give yourself the best chance of a happy marriage, you need to get the early days right to set the tone for your liaison. Micky added: 'You make more of an impression with someone in the first seconds, minutes or hours than you will for the rest of the time you know them. It's the same with a football club, you've got to make a good first impression, get a couple of quick wins.'

Day 3 – world class signs

I had listened closely to Micky during our summer meetings before my 100 days had begun as headteacher. Using the lessons I had learnt, I looked around the building before our teachers returned, before my Day 1, to see how I could achieve quick wins around the school.

To achieve that, I introduced new signage that highlighted our vision. Now, on every corridor, in every classroom and displayed on our stairwells, were messages of being 'world class'. The signs outlined our vision and articulated the sentiment through quotes from famous individuals who themselves had achieved great things. On Day 3, I referred to this signage in assemblies that reached out to every single student and member of staff in the school. It was a quick win to show a change in leadership and a shift in direction.

I could then support the messages they would see with a clear improvement plan. This plan was designed around our vision to become a 'world class school'. The plan was represented in an infographic that was displayed in every classroom. The aim here was to show not only where we were going but clearly how we would get there. This was inspired by the work Micky implemented in order to change the environment of the Tranmere training ground. We did not need a new uniform but we did need an ambitious look around the school.

Day 4 – the data never lies

On Day 4, I tried to exemplify the new standards I expected amongst our leadership team. I asked our team how our teaching staff accessed that data analysis required to monitor and intervene with under-performance amongst our students. This was very much akin to the question asked by Micky when he arrives at a club. While he introduced GPS tracking and a rigorous analytical approach to monitoring player performance in games and training, I changed our data analysis programme to one which could be more user friendly and insightful. In the days that followed, staff received training.

This new system reduced workload as the analysis could be easily accessed and conclusions could be drawn quicker. My personality is not one that naturally likes conflict. That can be a help and hindrance when you are looking to raise standards. I needed an approach that suited my personality but did the job. I have found that a calm, consistent and relentless approach to enhancing performance is my way.

The analysis of player performance improves standards. The system, used religiously across the board in the Premier League, is clear in how hard a player has worked, how many miles have been covered and how high their heart rate has been. Similarly, the new systematic and analytical approach to student performance meant that we could have open, honest and objective conversations with teachers and students. Once again, this was another quick win that represented a slicker approach to the way we reviewed what we do.

Sam Allardyce was one of the pioneers in this area. Micky and I had spoken about his approach in the week or so preceding my Day 1. Micky, as a former player for Sam, had sought to emulate this attention to detail. 'You just can't argue with things when they're really objective,' he explained. He continued: 'My players know I'm watching them. So they know that I'll know the second they drop their standards because it'll come through clearly on our analysis.' Sam moved away from being a manager who just based facts on his own opinion. He really led the way in this scientific approach. But he adds: 'You've still got to trust your eyes too. The GPS might not tell if a player is running like a headless chicken but it does ask a serious question if they've run a lot less than usual.'

The quick wins you can achieve can set the tone for the way you move forward. They have to be in keeping with your overall approach, your personality and the manner in which you intend to lead the organisation in the long run. With Micky's tough Glaswegian persona, I had perhaps expected to see his approach as distant and authoritarian. In fact, what I found was a man who led with relentlessly high standards that were underpinned by an analytical, objective but also empathetic approach. For any leader, establishing an objective and analytical approach that strives for success, while coupled with humility and empathy, can be a quick win that leads a team to success.

Credibility – find the big fish

First impressions, quick wins and early communication sets a trajectory. However, it is not the only transition point within the first 100 days.

The value of credibility per se has already been stressed by Mark Palios from a business perspective. Sam Allardyce explained that he recognises that getting that early credibility in football and leadership, particularly when you are an unknown as a leader, requires a keen eye for the individual. Allardyce explained: 'You've got to be able to pick out who the key people are in the dressing room. I have done it everywhere I've been. You need to quickly get a grip of the person that's going support you when there is some dissent in the dressing room and the person who'll stab you in the back given half a chance. I find the big fish, the one you've got to worry about, and I pick them up on something early on so they know the standards that we expect.'

Everett Rogers identified the types of people involved in his waves of change model. Top football managers work sub-consciously with players that fit each one of these personality types. Initially, the best managers that bring in ideas or innovations create a groundswell of support with the innovators. They are the players in the team eager for change and ready to work for the new manager. They are then followed by the early majority who will support the ideas of the early adopters and trust their opinions. Holding back are the late majority, the members of the team who have a touch of cynicism or lack the confidence to pledge support for a new manager. Finally are the laggards, the people who will either join the collective efforts and work with the new leadership or need to be moved on.

Innovation Adoption Lifecycle

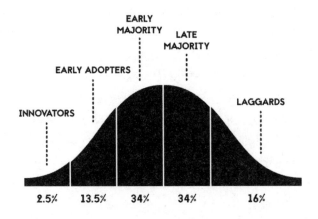

Professional football is perhaps a harder industry than most to establish credibility when you have not played the game at the same level as the players you are now leading. This was a challenge faced by Austin MacPhee, who took on the first team coaching role with Northern Ireland. Austin had not played the game at the top domestic level, let alone international level. He offered us a unique insight into gaining credibility.

'I reached a point where I got over the insecurity of not having a high-level playing career quickly and clearly. It came down to one key question that players ask themselves about a coach: 'Can they help me?' If the player believes you can help them improve or be more prepared to perform well due to the information you deliver, then the relationship will be good as long as you keep their trust and respect.'

Austin went on to talk about showing a conscious competence to gain trust and establish credibility. 'When I'm talking to top international players, I only say things that I know the purpose for. For example, I'll advise a top player to position themselves in a certain way so we can force a pass into a particular area. Top players will question that. So you've got to be able to give them an answer like: 'If we press the ball there, we force the pass here – where I have seen opposition turn the ball over frequently against this team.' You are not coaching them to play football. You are coaching them to play football in the system the manager is looking to employ.'

Players will appreciate that your point is based on evidence and you are not being authoritarian and saying: 'Do this because I say,' rather, 'do this because I have seen it will benefit you and the team.'

'It comes down to establishing credibility. Whether in business or football, I also believe that, when the opportunity allows, you need to try to develop relationships away from football. A stronger relationship builds trust and allows you to help players and staff more effectively. I think this can strengthen the bond with people and at international level it is really all you have.'

On the front foot – Moyes' men fit for the challenge

There are key principles to consider when setting out to achieve any quick win as a leader. These considerations can be easily remembered by using the acronym, AIM, which is; Appropriate, Important and Manageable.

AIM Model for Quick Wins

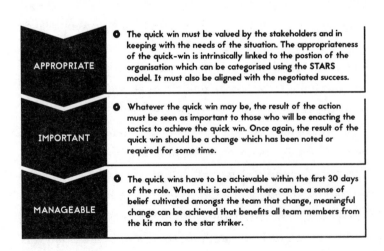

APPROPRIATE	● The quick win must be valued by the stakeholders and in keeping with the needs of the situation. The appropriateness of the quick-win is intrinsically linked to the postion of the organisation which can be categorised using the STARS model. It must also be aligned with the negotiated success.
IMPORTANT	● Whatever the quick win may be, the result of the action must be seen as important to those who will be enacting the tactics to achieve the quick win. Once again, the result of the quick win should be a change which has been noted or required for some time.
MANAGEABLE	● The quick wins have to be achievable within the first 30 days of the role. When this is achieved there can be a sense of belief cultivated amongst the team that change, meaningful change can be achieved that benefits all team members from the kit man to the star striker.

In an attempt to understand what can make or break the first week for a football manager, Micky spoke to a man who had arguably the toughest challenge of all – filling the shoes of Sir Alex Ferguson. The man with this almost impossible task was David Moyes. Micky and I were interested to hear what Moyes had learnt from his experiences at Manchester United and how he used those lessons in his two stints as manager of West Ham United.

'We needed to make an immediate impact. That is what was required if West Ham were to avoid losing their place in the Premier League,' said Moyes, referring back to his first spell in charge of the Hammers.

Talking about the fitness of the players, Moyes was quoted in an article in the *Independent* during those early days in charge in November 2017 as saying: 'We might need to upset a few people to get where we want to go.' In conversation with Micky, he went on to say: 'I recognised this was a turnaround situation and I'd gained knowledge of current fitness levels. You need those early wins to get the momentum and then in the game, win or lose, you can show them the sprints have increased, the stamina has increased and you hope that, with all that, you'll be able to say that the results have improved. Fortunately, at West Ham, we could say that and those first few days of my first 100 at the club really got us moving in the right direction.'

Moyes explained how the perilous position of the club simplified the initial objectives that were set. 'The negotiation of success was straightforward, the owners needed survival in the Premier League. The success also needed to be negotiated with the players as well. The position of the team, though, gave me some licence to move things around quickly and demand instant change, which you sometimes do not have the luxury of when you go to a bigger club that has been doing quite well.'

Moyes was able to point to the statistical evidence that West Ham's players needed to increase their work rate if they expected to turn around their fortunes. 'The evidence, the success criteria and the personal pride of all involved with the club provided me with the platform for change,' explained Moyes. 'They made the need for a change in approach, which resulted in a more physically fit side. This change needed to be achieved quickly so, in that sense, I needed to show that this was manageable once the importance and the way in which we'd go about doing things were made clear to all concerned. In order to execute this quick win, early training sessions were physically demanding.'

The quick win gave Moyes the platform to drive West Ham to 13th in the Premier League as they ensured their Premier League survival with two games to spare. He achieved nine wins and 10 draws from 31 games and stabilised a club that appeared to be spiralling toward relegation from the Premier League, which would have been a catastrophic blow. Moyes managed to achieve this success despite losing three first team players in the January transfer window and bringing in only one new addition, Jordan Hugill, who was a player with potential rather than proven quality in England's elite league.

For Moyes, his approach to taking on such a challenge has

changed with experience. 'At West Ham, I carried out the due diligence which allowed me to pinpoint the key issue in the performance of the team. I made it really clear to everyone that my vision, if you like, was to win games. I knew that this was only about winning and not a long-term project.'

As such, he effectively analysed the club's position, negotiated success effectively with the board and then executed the actions which would allow him to achieve the success that had be agreed upon before a ball was kicked.

Day 5 – seeing is believing

At St Bede's, I spent a lot of time in that first week observing the movements of students and staff in and out of the classroom. It led me to understand that the first issue I had to tackle was that of relationships between students and some staff. It appeared to me that there was a disconnect which I felt needed to change. I did this by taking on more duties around school, allowing for more interaction.

At the end of that first week, while there is not a media spotlight like at a football club, there is a spotlight that casts a judgement just as quickly – the parents. This feedback was coming back positive.

A governor of the school pulled me to one side at the end of Day 5 and said: 'I asked one of the parents what people thought of you and they said, 'My daughter says she sees him a lot around the school. It seems like he's everywhere. He smiles and asks us if we're ok. I like that. I think we're seeing the other teachers doing that more too. So well done.'

Day 7 – using sport to break down barriers

This was a positive start but I also wanted to get an understanding of the thoughts of the older, sometimes more challenging students and their parents. By the end of Day 7, I had a general momentum with the staff and students and also wins with key students across the school.

We had an issue of some poor behaviour on the yard which gave me the opportunity to call meetings with several of the culture-setting students and their parents. They were expecting a telling off and some of their parents approached a meeting with me defensively. But I spoke to them about the behaviours I had seen and the impression that it gave me, which was one of them being disaffected with the school. I asked them and their parents how we could work together to change that. They said they were bored in their free time and this caused them to act in the way they had been. Their parents agreed and said they felt they just needed to let off steam. We then discussed how we could make that happen.

The boys all said they would like more sport. So I arranged that. I personally supervised a weekly indoor football session. Again, this showed our culture-setting students I would work with them but I would not accept poor behaviour. It gave me a chance to stand and talk to them every week while they played football. This early win proved crucial. Now the loudest and biggest students in the school, metaphorically and literally, were onside and understood how I would be leading this school, with high expectations but an understanding ear. I really took so much from the words of David Moyes here.

'Go, see and understand' – and a derby day rant

As well as the great opportunities that come from quick wins there are also potential pitfalls. Many leaders fall foul of an overzealous approach which fails to take into account the situational environment in an attempt to achieve 'quick wins'.

Micky explained that when he arrived at Tranmere, he did not make the mistake of bringing in an 'off-the-shelf' strategy that may have worked somewhere else. He watched. He listened. He observed. 'I resisted the temptation to get drawn into the detail of the approach to training, the club infrastructure and the culture,' he told me.

As Micky took his time, the players grew more curious about what his approach would be. His first words were chosen deliberately in terms of their sentiment and their timing. It was a derby between Tranmere and Wrexham, a fiercely fought contest between two sides on opposite sides of the Welsh/English border. 'As the players arrived at the ground they had spent a week preparing without any input from me,' said Micky. 'They thought I was just an observer. I was never an observer, in fact I was an analyst, an inspector and a judge of all that I had seen.' The players prepared for the game in a relaxed fashion and as they returned to the dressing room for their final preparations before the derby began, Micky's reign began.

The new boss had seen enough. 'The players had been listening to music, laughing and joking. I didn't see that passion or that fire that you need on a derby day. I spoke for the first time to the entire group and let them have it.

This was a derby game and they were all acting like they were about to go on holiday at the airport. I laid into them and the shock factor worked.'

Crucially, Micky did not utter those words at the beginning of the week without perhaps the weight of his observations to back-up his impressions of a group lacking in focus and a mentality to succeed at all costs. He had absorbed all that had gone before him that week and now, using his own principles and philosophy, he would begin an approach that would turnaround the team and the club's fortunes over the next season and a half. Tranmere won 1-0 that day and it signalled the beginning of an impressive unbeaten run. That season Rovers would accrue a club record 95 points and surpass several other club milestones. The support base turned almost immediately from a frustrated, downbeat collective to an optimistic, rejuvenated force that saw the future rather than the glories of the past.

As I headed home after seven days in my new role, I spoke with Micky about his approach to his first week. I was interested to know where exactly these ideas had come from. Micky explained to me over my hands-free phone that he developed this approach through a deep study of the Toyota car company. I was amazed. He explained: 'Toyota's approach is 'go, see and understand without preconception,' which translates as *Genchi Genbutsu*.' By this point of getting to know Micky, the fact that a football manager was now explaining Japanese management systems was an unexpected twist in our efforts to investigate the topic of leadership in the first 100 days.

'You basically look around the place and ask yourself why we do things this way. You don't just accept things the way they are. You go, see and understand it,' Micky explained. I did my own research following this as I wanted to get a detailed understanding of where this Toyota theory came from. I read about Taiichi Ohno, considered to be the father of the Toyata Production System, who is quoted in the Toyota Way document as stating: 'Observe the production floor without preconceptions and with a blank mind. Repeat 'why' five times to every matter.'

Burnley questionnaire – get inside their heads

Sean Dyche was another manager who practised the approach of 'go, see and understand' as he went about getting under the skin of the club.

As we sipped some fantastic coffee from the sort of coffee machine you would expect at a Premier League club, he explained the way in which he captured the opinions of the players.

'In those early days, I gave the players a questionnaire. They could give them back anonymously. Although some did write their names on them, I wasn't bothered about who was saying what. I just wanted to understand what they thought of themselves and what they thought others thought about them. Then I'd compare that to my opinions to see if there were any gaps.

'I asked them stuff like: 'Are you fit? Do you think you're playing well? What do you think of yourself? What do others think of you?' Pretty open questions really but it allowed me to get an understanding of where the players' minds were at as a group. Up until that point, I'd seen a couple of games and watched from the outside, but I didn't have a good understanding of them as individuals. Getting their input early on gave me a clearer idea on what I needed to do to get the kind of club and culture I knew would make Burnley successful again.'

As I listened to Sean speak, I couldn't help but think back to those 'take no prisoners' leaders who often go in and rip everything apart and start all over again. The 'their way or no way' approach which can bring about short-term results but rarely has a sustained impact. All too often these approaches, which ignore the people and positives of an organisation, can be damaging for elements of culture such as trust, respect and a sense of team. It was clear from our time with Sean that he did indeed move people on who weren't of the necessary mindset or quality but he did it in keeping with his genuine persona. This allowed for an authentic culture to develop at Burnley in a sustained way.

Prepare for the storms

Sir Alex Ferguson, in his book 'Leading', explains how he changed his approach to the proverbial 'trouble'. He states how in his early days at St Mirren and then Aberdeen, he would proactively look for problems or issues. He would look for the dissenters in the dressing room or make pains to find out who was painting the town red the night before training or, worse, before a game. When he arrived at Manchester United, his approach changed. Ferguson waited for the conflict, the battle or the misdemeanours to find him. If issues were not affecting the performance on the training ground or the pitch, they were not a priority. However, what Ferguson was certain of, despite this change in approach, was that if you do not look for trouble, it will come to find you.

Like leaders in any sphere, football managers will face obstacles, criticism and possible rebellion. Unlike leaders in other spheres these challenges can be very public and high profile. The player who storms off the pitch, kicking the water bottles and throwing his shirt amongst other disillusioned substitutes, can create a sense of dressing room discontent and suggest a player mutiny.

Such a display of public defiance can be a PR nightmare for managers who realise that not only do the cameras see such behaviour but also the supporters, players and club owners. The thrown shirt or a petulant arm thrown in the direction of a football manager is a visible challenge to authority in a heated moment. Leaders in all walks of life can be sure of one thing; if they are challenging people and demanding high standards, they too will receive a metaphorical shirt thrown in their direction during the course of their tenure. Indeed, what can be even more of a challenge is the silent critic, the dressing room or staff room terrorist that can be silent but culturally deadly.

In order to counter the possible derailment of the leader, there must be a considered approach which acknowledges that challenge to leadership will occur. Later in the book, we will look at motivation and alignment strategies that tackle the challenges. At this point, strategies can be employed that engage the head rather than the heart.

Step 1 – Predict the challenges over the season

By asking the team, what are the likely challenges over the course of this season, both collectively and individually, the manager can agree a set of principles. For example, when a player is not selected there is a sense of indignation, embarrassment and perhaps even humiliation for the individual not selected. This will happen over the course of the season.

The same emotions can also be equated to a scenario whereby a player is substituted during a game. Rather than the former example, the latter example is played out in front of thousands of supporters which only adds intensity to the situation. Knowing that this situation will occur over the course of a season and mutually appreciating the emotive response such an occurrence elicits is something which can be factored into a manager's planning.

Step 2 – Hammer time? Anticipate conflict

Managers such as David Moyes and Micky both share their approach to these situations which is to establish agreed behaviours before the event occurs. Micky, for example, agreed with his players that if they were told on Friday that they were not selected for the game on the Saturday, then they should wait until Monday until addressing this with the manager.

The team, both management and playing staff, agreed that this was mutually beneficial. It allows the player a period of time to be calm before raising their frustrations and it also allows the manager to get on with the job of preparing the team rather than dealing with the distraction in the heat of the moment.

David Moyes, while at West Ham, had a similar agreement with players when they were substituted. Moyes asked the players how they felt they should react when being substituted. The players agreed that they should act respectfully and raise the issue at a later date should they feel the need to. To not do so could damage the team and distract from the objective, which is to win the game at hand. In both cases, when the rules were broken, the manager could then discipline the player, referring back to the agreed behaviours set out at the beginning of the season.

For leaders of any kind, it is crucial to predict the conflict and agree avenues through which complaints or concerns could be raised. It is crucial for any organisation that wishes to have systems that encourage continuous development that all members of the team, club and organisation have a voice which can be heard.

At St Bede's, we now actively encouraged all members of our staff team to talk to the line managers, senior leaders or their union representatives in order that everyone could feel like their voice matters.

Step 3 – Sir Alex and the kung-fu kick – calm control

Once the ground rules have been set after being inextricably linked to the objective, then the consequence must be followed through consistently in order to maintain a firm but fair approach. The discussions following an infringement on the agreed rules can then be objective and, while individuals may often not agree, they are more likely to concede that a consequence is fair. Just as importantly, the dressing room is also more likely to acknowledge a fair consequence to the behaviour.

Throughout his book 'Leading', Sir Alex Ferguson gives many examples of dealing with indiscipline in a consistent but supportive manner. He gives a detailed description of the ban that followed Eric Cantona's infamous 'kung-fu kick' attack on a Crystal Palace fan in 1995. Ferguson explains how the club had punished Cantona but then offered him a great deal of support during his eight-month ban. As a result, despite the ban, Cantona resisted the temptations of playing in Italy in order to remain at United.

Ferguson stresses that while he had very high standards, he dealt with the players with respect and did not hold grudges. But he made it very clear that failure to live up to the high standards of the organisation would ultimately lead to them leaving the club.

Moving on

After the excitement of the first week, it was crucial to ensure those early positives were quickly supported by actions that achieved quick wins.

Using the strategies of many top managers, I believed a momentum had been created around the school. I thought of these initial weeks a little bit like the take-off of a plane. Micky and I talked about how that initial planning and preparation is followed by the excitement of lift-off. During Week 1 you are just leaving the ground and looking up into the heavens above. The remaining weeks of Month 1 then see the rapid ascent on a steep trajectory. The speed is quick and so the slightest bump or pocket of air can seem like significant turbulence. However, quick wins can gain a confidence amongst the team that this journey will be a safe and successful one. An impression like this can gain the confidence of the team.

However, Micky was quick to temper what, in hindsight, was over-confidence at the success of my take-off. During a morning commute call he reminded me: 'Don't forget, you've not dropped anyone yet. You've not told anyone they're not good enough. You've not had to deliver a message they don't want to hear. When you do, then you'll know how well you're doing.'

He was not wrong. What lay ahead would be internal and external challenges that would seriously test this leadership approach.

Reflections

1. Where does the organisation need quick wins?

2. How can you manage to achieve these wins?

3. Why are these wins important?

4. How will you know when you have achieved them?

5. Who are your innovators, early adopters, late adopters and laggards?

6. How will you systematically go, see and understand?

7. What are your predictable challenges?

8. *How can you set up a conversation around establishing agreed behaviours in the tough times?*
9. *What will the consequences of breaking these rules be?*
10. *What will be the rewards to following these rules?*

130

Chapter Five

DAY 8-19

 All aboard the team bus

United we stand – systems and suits

The feel-good factor was back at Manchester United, one week after Ole Gunnar Solskjær had been handed the role. 'Training was fresh and bright. We had brought an identity back to the club,' explained Mick Phelan. There were further victories over the Christmas period against Huddersfield, Bournemouth, Newcastle and Reading. United scored 16 goals in those first five matches with a 4-3-3 attacking style that brought joy and excitement back to the club. That said, Ole knew that they could not operate like this against high quality opposition. The next opponents were Tottenham Hotspur, away from home at Wembley Stadium. It would be their toughest test yet.

Prior to the trip, the team went away to Dubai for a warm weather training camp which both Ole and Mick identify as being a turning point in the players' belief in their ability to do the job on a permanent basis.

'During our trip to Dubai we made two big changes. The first one was our system for the game against Tottenham,' explained Ole. It was not the system as such that was a turning point – changing from 4-3-3 to a diamond formation with split strikers – it was the way in which this decision was reached that was significant. 'I was sat with Marcus (Rashford), Jesse (Lingard) and Anthony (Martial) and we were talking about how we would play against Tottenham. We involved them in making the decisions. When we used that system and we won, then the guys are thinking, 'These lot know what they're doing. They're not just going to make us happy, they're going to help us win.' That was massive for our first 100 days.'

Ole and Mick had timed it perfectly. They spent their first month developing relationships and reigniting the cultures and traditions of Manchester United. Crucially, Ole did not just expect this momentum to continue, he used it as a platform for longer-term improvement. The timing was right, the foundations of his leadership had been quickly established from the opening day messages and the staff Christmas party. Now, with credibility established, he had begun to make changes to the style of play and shifted the ownership of decisions throughout the team.

'The second big thing we did was bring back the suits. At first, the players weren't keen. Getting them to wear a shirt and tie wasn't the easiest. But, when they walked into Wembley with those blazers on with that badge on it, those Tottenham players looked at them and thought, 'I want to play for Manchester United," explained Ole. 'It was important we did that,' echoed Mick Phelan, 'because it brought back the identity even more. All those players that had gone before wearing that badge and that blazer, you can't help but feel that when you're wearing it.'

In these two moments, Ole and Mick had brought about a new way of thinking in a devolved leadership style. Players, coaching staff, support staff and anyone who cared to speak, now had a voice. The group of players wearing the red jerseys were now becoming more like Manchester United players and the fans could see that. When United now arrived at away games, they looked like the teams of the past in their sharp, business-like attire. The tone had been set within the first 30 days.

This approach was authentic and the two men meant what they said about their feelings toward Manchester United. Similarly, Shelley Kerr developed relationships with the Scotland women's team by being clear that she did not see the Scotland national team as 'her' side. She explained how the senior players influenced the values of the squad. Shelley described the process: 'I started by saying that this was not my team. This was a national team and we had to set our values. I said to them that they need to set the values as a squad. We said we wanted to be more entertaining. We said we solved problems together and we'll make mistakes together. It got a lot of buy-in from the entire team.'

Shelley has undeniable emotional intelligence which has enabled her to develop powerful relationships with every group she has led. She spoke to me about these '360 degree' relationships: 'It's a difficult challenge because you're the key decision maker and you have to make decisions that will upset people. You have to remember that you are not in control of winning a match, you can influence it but you cannot control that. As a national manager, you have to build relationships with clubs; give their players the best care and attention while they are away with the national team. The national side is difficult because you've got a limited time with 23 players. So I have to focus on the objective and the process.'

Shelley went on to explain how she relates to the wider stakeholders in the national games. 'On a regular basis, I have dialogue with the Scottish FA. I speak to people about the travel, commercial side, youth development and so on.' At the core of Shelley's approach, and for that matter of Ole and Mick, was a consistent awareness of the people who influence the performance of her team on the pitch and the long-term development of the women's game in Scotland.

A road full of peaks and troughs

School budgets do not stretch to team-building trips to Dubai. However, with the first seven days in my new role now behind me, I believed I had the momentum of a good start. My chats with Micky after this initial period were always tempered by his analogies such as: 'You don't win anything in August.' This old football adage urges caution to any players, managers or supporters who may become overly confident after an early couple of wins in the league. It was now crucial for me to begin a process which was much longer-term than those early quick wins. This process was leading a school which had everyone on the bus and looking in the right direction.

Day 8-19: All Aboard The Team Bus

The life of a football manager involves moments of excitement, deflation, exhilaration, anxiety and euphoria. The road that is travelled, full of peaks and troughs, is taken both literally and metaphorically on the team bus.

The modern-day team bus can be luxurious yet, like the school buses of our childhood, it can be a political minefield. The conversations, the seating position of the star players, the cliques and the outsiders on board make up an intriguing mix. Some of the passengers will be looking forward, down the road, awaiting the destination with anticipation and belief. Some could be seeking out a negative cohesion or a compassionate ear to vent their frustrations to – perhaps of perceived rejection or being overlooked. Others await the destination to see if it is what they had expected or demanded. For teams in the business or education world, this bus is metaphorical, however these dynamics exist in every company, school or department. There will always be people in the team or the wider club that buy into the manager's vision wholeheartedly. Conversely, there will always be those who feel uncomfortable with it and for a variety of reasons may actively seek to sabotage it. Finally, there will be those in between who await to see how this journey will affect them or how their influential peers will view the transition.

Ole and Mick could relate to this complexity as they had been landed, as described earlier, with a mixture of players at various stages of their career. As they considered their team bus, as all leaders must do, they viewed the picture with a high degree of emotional intelligence.

Day 10 – the captains in my team

On my 10th day in the role, we had a visit from a teaching union. At the time, there was no union representation amongst the staff, which the union were well aware of. They explained to me that the meeting would be solely to share information. By the time they left, we had four union representatives amongst our staff! I have since come to realise that we are the only school in the country which supports four reps from the same union.

However, I quickly worked with the new union reps to ensure that they were not only on board the bus but they had a real sense of their importance in planning our journey together. I explained the pivotal nature of union reps to Micky as this was perhaps a difference between our two sectors – although, of course, the Professional Footballers' Association, among other organisations, has long been established. 'Really, they're like your captains,' Micky suggested over one of our commuting chats which were akin to mentoring sessions. 'Treat them like your captains. Imagine the influence they can have amongst your team. Imagine if you could actually harness that influence…'

My approach was immediately one of consultation and consideration. I spoke with our new union reps about their role in gathering the thoughts of all staff and sharing that with me as they saw fit. I trusted the individuals to filter out the moans and groans from the real concerns. What you can be sure of is that any team or office will have issues. If people are given a transparent way of sharing these issues then open conversations can be had about improving efficiency.

Ultimately, we all have appraisal targets, a clear purpose and an expected level of performance, whether that's the number of goals scored or the results of a teacher's class. If you can create a climate where the team feel heard and valued, there is a real cohesion and collective effort that can thrive.

A captain, as Micky stressed to me, is pivotal in creating such an environment. 'I've always had a captain who will come and tell me if there's something going on I need to know about. Someone who I can trust to filter out the rubbish, tell people to get on with it if they're moaning but also confident enough to come and tell me if there's a real issue in the camp. That's what your captain should be there for. That's what your union reps can be for you.'

He was absolutely spot on. Since Day 10, we have established a great working relationship. Not only are our meetings productive but other meetings and discussions, such as strategic middle leader meetings, are not bogged down with issues around union guidance because we have separate time to discuss those issues.

Micky's advice was clear and it is advice which all leaders must follow: know who the captains of your team are. Make sure they are telling you what is going on at the back of your team bus, around the water cooler or in the staff room.

A good captain is a key link. Far from listening to the trepidation fellow heads shared with me about union reps, I have embraced the thoughts and challenge from these talented individuals who are leaders themselves and treated them like the captains of our team.

Getting the right people on the bus

Ole, Sam Allardyce, Joe Royle and Micky see getting the right people on board his team bus as integral to his role as a football leader. In education, recruitment happens later in the year for teachers and so you are limited, during the first 100 days, in your ability to change personnel. However, there was still opportunity for me to make changes to roles and later in the year, it was possible to recruit people I knew would add value to our team.

Giving the right message to these new recruits is crucial in the selection process. I need my prospective staff to understand our culture and ambition before they commit themselves to our school and certainly before we, as a school, commit to employing them. I was fascinated to hear just how Micky evaluated his players on the bus and the process he went through to recruit new players. Over a curry at the end of another busy week, Micky shared his approach with me.

Day 15 – Socrates and footballers

As Micky knows, the demands on the players he recruits will be high. He knows that it is easy to be swayed by the sales pitches of agents and intermediaries. Micky and I met with the Technical Director of the League Managers Association, Dr Wayne Allison, at St George's Park, home of the English national team. Famously nicknamed 'the Chief', fans of many clubs will remember Wayne from his long and successful football career, in which he played for nine clubs between 1987 and 2008.

Over lunch, our conversation turned to recruitment. Both Wayne and Micky shared a belief that this is a facet of leadership in football and beyond which can make or break a manager's career. 'We often sit in silence for a few moments,' Micky explained, 'the players look at me and I look at them. I wait. In these moments of silence, sometimes tension, I'm looking for the player to start telling me what they want. If they don't start by saying why they are here and why they want to play for me, I might just walk out. You need to know that the players you're recruiting have a passion and a desire to improve and help you win games for the football club. I'll then ask them 'why?' a few times.'

In education, we describe this method of drilling down as Socratic questioning. Usually asking 'why?' five times gets to the route of the reason for any behaviour, whether that be asking why a child is late for school, why a business deal has gone wrong or why a player wants to play for a football club. Micky continued: 'If I don't get the sense that they're here to improve for themselves and they don't see me as someone that can help them do that, then I'll cut the meeting short. If they're sitting down and saying to me, 'make me better', then there's a good chance the negotiations will work out well.'

Joe Royle was famous for his astute recruitment. 'It got to a point where I was wanting to speak with clubs about young players they had coming through or that they were about to release and they'd be saying 'no' because I'd see the potential before they did. You've got to have eyes and ears everywhere so that you can get the right people on board the team bus. You're looking for people with a hunger to do well and you just can't coach that hunger. They've got to want to do well for themselves and for the football club.' Beyond football, leaders must challenge potential new recruits to immediately understand and get on board with the direction of the bus.

At Ormiston Chadwick Academy, Tuesday Humby takes a similar approach to recruiting the right people for the bus. When she recruits new members for her teaching team, she shows them around the school and gives them a clear message. 'I tell them they'll work harder here than they'll work anywhere else. I tell them they will need to do long hours and that they probably won't sleep for the first few weeks. Then I tell them about the back story of some of our pupils. They get to know how hard some of our kids have it and how they need people who won't give up on them.'

Tuesday knows some candidates will walk away at the thought of this. She is fully aware that this is not the glossy sales pitch that many schools can offer.

However, what she does know is that it if the candidates apply and come back, then they are the sort of people she can work with. They buy in to the cause and are the right people for her bus. This approach is not dissimilar to the newspaper advert taken out by Sir Ernest Shackleton prior to his South Pole expedition.

Shackleton printed a statement in the papers, to the effect of this: *Men wanted for hazardous journey to the South Pole. Small wages, bitter cold, long months of complete darkness, constant danger. Safe return doubtful. Honour and recognition in case of success.*

In essence, with an honest, purpose-driven recruitment approach, the right people are more likely to come on board the bus. For the Scotland national women's team, Shelley Kerr has a process-driven system for recruitment. 'I've got a criteria based on attitude, application and performance. I have a grid with the key things required,' she explained. 'Performance relates to being able to cope under pressure and follow tactical instructions. Attitude is all about the person and within each of the three pillars there are other set things we are looking for.'

For Shelley and her coaching team, this is part of a bigger picture. 'It's a way of working, from recruitment to the frameworks that we use for analysis, training and matchday preparation. There's continuity within the way we deliver.' Interestingly, the players are fully aware of this approach which provides rationale for every action. 'In international football, you have small windows with the players so the focus is on a framework that makes it easier to just hit the ground running. In a club environment, I might be more flexible in the way I approach things because I'd have time to do that.'

When Jim Collins and his research team studied what made a team move from being good to great, in his book of the same title, they were surprised with the most important factor for development. They found that getting the right people on the bus was more important than where the bus was going and how it was going to get there. For the football manager, getting the right people on the bus is fundamental to a successful first 100 days for three key reasons.

The first reason is that having the right people on the bus allows for teams to adapt to an ever-changing world. Football managers need players who are prepared to cope with challenges throughout the season. They require players and staff that can deal with success in a composed and humble manner. Equally, they require players and staff that can be resilient and determined when results go against the club or if they personally are dropped or substituted. In other walks of life, this is the same. If the right people are on the bus, they will be able to deal with each permutation with a positive perspective and a belief that the leadership will continue the development of the team.

The second key reason for the right people on the bus is that the problem of motivation is largely redundant. Sam Allardyce is certainly a manager who believes that. 'If you need to motivate a player for Manchester United away then you are in big trouble. You've got to get people who are ready for the challenge. I'd look at every bit of information I could get hold of to get the most informed profile of a player. You're saving yourself a lot of trouble down the line if you get that bit right.'

As a leader of a school, this has certainly resonated with me as I perhaps was of the belief that motivation was of principle importance. While strategies of reinforcing belief are important to sustain growth, motivation per se is perhaps surprisingly low down the list of pivotal factors in the first 100 days. Rather, the key aspect is assessing the people already on the bus and if required – and if possible – getting new people on board.

Thirdly, and perhaps most simply, if you have an ambitious and exciting vision then the wrong people will simply not be able to realise this ambition. Micky has attracted players willing to play at lower levels for lower wages because of his offer. 'I care about the players I recruit. It's not about me, it's really not. I tell them what I think they're good at and how I believe I can improve them. As a leader, you get people knowing you've got their interests at heart and that you've a love for them. You've got to follow through on that then but there's a promise between you that you'll both give your all to help each other. I know there are players who've said: 'Go and play for him because he'll improve you,' even when there've been offers of more money somewhere else. You approach things like that and you'll get the players thinking about improving as people and players more than just thinking about the pay packet. I can tell them, and show them examples, of how I've improved players who've gone on to play at higher levels and then got all that monetary reward which is important to anyone in their career.'

Character, competence, chemistry – recruit right

During the first 30 days of turnaround or organisation leadership, Mark Palios works with his HR department to develop an effective team. He explains how he gains an insight into his key personnel. 'After a month, I've sat down with the key leaders in the organisation and I will ask them where they want to be in the next five years. If someone hasn't got the ambition, then that's a problem. I'd say to them that if they give me two years of their life, I'll give them a better CV.' Palios then referenced President Kennedy who asked a cleaner what his job was. The cleaner famously replied: 'To put a man on the moon.' Palios used this analogy to express his belief that everyone in the organisation should have a sense of ambition and a belonging to the collective purpose of the group. The emotional intelligence of Palios was clear. He was also completely consistent in his focus on people, money and time.

Drew Povey, who is a leadership consultant to several blue chip companies having previously been a leader in education and elite sport, offers a straightforward but effective approach to recruitment. 'It's based on the principle of three C's; character, competence and chemistry.

The recruitment strategies of Micky, Royle and Allardyce all follow the principles of this model,' Povey explained to me during a game at Prenton Park.

The Three C's of Recruitment

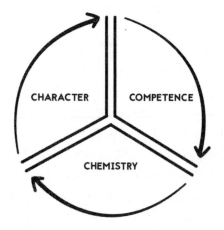

He continued, 'Firstly, you need to focus on character. You need to make sure that you're recruiting people with the right attitudes and behaviours for your team. Character is really difficult to develop in someone so save yourself a lot of time in the long run and make sure your recruitment deep dives into potential employees' character. Secondly, competence is crucial. The people you bring in need to have the ability, the skill-set and the potential for growth. If you've got someone with the right character, you can make a real difference in a person's competence. Conversely, if you've got someone with the wrong character they might have the competence but not necessarily the inclination to utilise this competence. Finally, it's down to chemistry. You've got to ask if the person will fit into the group when we consider the team dynamic. That's down to the balance you're looking for. Often in sport you're looking for a blend of youth and experience but in any organisation you need to consider how all of the 'players' will fit together.'

Drew went on to say that he believes that recruitment has been affected by the world health crisis. 'Recruitment in many organisations used to be all about IQ, then it moved to EQ but now I think there's such a massive importance on AQ. AQ is Adaptive Quota. Someone's ability to evolve is just as important as EQ and IQ, if not more so,' explained Drew. He went on: 'The people that can shift and move to the ever-changing landscapes are the ones who'll thrive now. You've got to be humble to be adaptive, though. You don't have all the answers and the moment you believe you do, you instantly start limiting your potential.'

Drew then explained his morning physical and mental workout. 'I'm obsessed with learning. I read books and articles on leadership so that I am constantly honing my craft as a coach, writer and speaker. I never think I'm done and that I know it all. Every morning I do a physical workout, then my breathing exercises and then I devote half an hour to leadership reading. It keeps me fresh and constantly learning.' In a world where nothing is certain, we need people in our teams who are able to react and respond to changing resources, goals and expectations.

These words rang in my ears when I had chance to recruit new staff beyond the first 100 days. In one particular case, we had a day of interviews that involved four very strong candidates. It was a teaching job and in the classroom there were probably two stronger candidates than the successful applicant. What made the difference was the successful individual's desire to improve, their understanding of our culture and their commitment to being a part of our ambitious drive to fulfil our world class vision. I opted to employ this individual because their skills were enough of a base to get started but their alignment would mean they could improve the school beyond their classroom.

'I shouldn't have done it – he made me so angry'

Micky subscribes to a simple traffic light assessment of the players on his team bus. The end result is a RAG (i.e. red, amber, green) rating of the player. 'Those with green ratings are the ones we believed to be well capable of supporting the drive for success. Those with amber ratings were a risk, have potential or are unproven. Those in red are probably not quite ready for that desired level or they're not playing at the standard we need to reach the goal. That doesn't mean that people that aren't quite there are redundant. Quite often they help as part of the squad but if they believe they should be in the first team and you don't see that, then you've got to have those tough conversations.'

Although there may be those within a team with whom the leader may clash, it is important that as Sam Allardyce puts it, you 'don't cut your nose off to spite your face'. He explains: 'The people in the building, on the pitch or within the organisation must be worked with initially. You've got to quickly assess whether you think you can improve people and if not, then you need a plan to change things.' Allardyce, through the experience of working at a variety of clubs, is acutely aware that people behave in ways that are determined by recent experiences, perceptions that may be misleading and a multitude of other reasons that are only human. What one can be sure of is that, unless they are divisive or dangerous to the organisation in an extreme sense, you must work with them in order to understand their potential and bring the best out of them.

Sean Dyche shared with us a story from his early days at Burnley when dealing with players that wanted away from the club but were still required, until the end of his first season, to give all they had on the pitch. 'I remember one player who had been in the press saying how great he thought I was and how we were really looking good this year in my first season at Burnley. I knew, though, that he'd been talking with another manager and he was trying to get himself out of the club. It's one of my only regrets as a manager, and I don't have many, but I pulled him on it. We were walking back from training and I clocked he was on his own, so I said 'I've seen the stuff you've put in the paper' and he said 'it's great gaffer, what do you think?' So I told him: 'I think it's a load of rubbish. You know and I know that you're trying to get a move out of here."

Dyche continued: 'I shouldn't have done it. I wouldn't do it again but he'd made me so angry I felt I needed to say something. In hindsight it was difficult to get him back online, we did in the end and he did ok for us but I learnt from that. Note to self – don't do that again.'

What was interesting about this story was that it is so tempting sometimes, as leaders, to address certain issues in a vitriolic way as being undermined can unearth an almost primal fury because of a lack of respect. With experience, Dyche adopts a more considered, almost neutral approach to issues like the one he faced.

One way in which the manager can begin to unpick the reason for an individual's negative behaviours or apparent disdain for the transitional period is to assess the basis of their motivation, their psychological state and their key drivers.

Assessing motivation – Vardy's anger

Many football managers we spoke to during the writing of this book believed that motivation was an internal job with external consequences. Big Sam and Micky both agreed that motivation is something which largely comes from within over the long-term but that a leader can offer short-term motivation for bursts of 15-20 minutes, in a match for example. However, motivating a group of individuals is something that is driven by their strong sense of 'why'. Establishing a collective 'why' and engaging a group in this shared cause was discussed at length earlier in the book. There are also contributing factors within an organisation which can fertilise this 'why' or this sense of purpose.

Dyche has changed his beliefs around motivation and morality. Addressing Micky during our wide-ranging discussion, he said: 'In our day, we'd play for the shirt, the pride and because we loved it. Nowadays, players might be playing for a Ferrari or to become a millionaire. That used to bother me but I've caught myself on now. If a player comes to me and says, 'I want to get a Ferrari', I'll say, 'Ok, I'll help you get that but you need to work hard to be able to do that.' Some people play for material things, others for their family, it doesn't really matter to me anymore. I've just got to tap into their motivation and let them know that I'm here to help them get that. That said, they've got to give everything they've got to me and the team in order to get the prize they want.'

Dyche is a leader who inspired players, supporters and arguably an entire town to believe in his authentic approach. 'When the players see you're helping them out and looking to help them personally or develop them professionally they'll give you that extra bit the majority of the time. You might get the clever ones who think they'll take advantage of that but nine times out of 10 they won't. What will happen is that if the other lads see that happening they'll pull their team-mates up on it and tell them they're being out of order. Then you've got a dressing room who are giving their all for you. If they're going to take advantage and muck about, they'll do it anyway, regardless of the manager's approach.'

Micky is widely acknowledged to be a motivational master. Perhaps his most famous discovery was a prime example of how he finds the key to a player's motivation.

Jamie Vardy is now an England international, the 2020 Premier League Golden Boot winner, a Premier League title winner and has received the Premier League Player of the Season Award. Micky signed Vardy while he was at non-league Fleetwood. In terms of his motivation, Micky believes he saw it clearly. 'Vardy's motivation was anger. He could turn anger into energy. He could turn anger into performance. He used what was almost like an inner fury to get to that ball first or press that ball harder than anyone else. I've followed his career and since the time he was with me until now, he is at his most dangerous when he's angry. When people doubt him or criticise him, that gives him the fuel of anger. He's unplayable at times when he's angry. Anger can be free energy or free fuel.' Finding an individual's motivation, like with Vardy, is vital to releasing potential and commitment.

In his *New York Times* top 10 bestseller book, 'Drive', Dan Pink dissects the three pillars of motivation. Pink is an expert in economic transformation and the new workplace at corporations, associations and universities. The three pillars he ascribes to are: autonomy, mastery and purpose. If we look at these three areas individually, it is possible to develop an audit of individuals' motivation across an organisation. It is also clear that many football managers have carried out a similar exercise in order to assess the motivational state of the group.

Autonomy: When Pink refers to this, he refers to an independent motivation driven by choice. If we imagine motivation like a fire, then it must be given fuel, heat and oxygen. Individuals must be given the space, resources and tempered pressure to perform. Autonomous motivation can be facilitated but it cannot be enforced. Pink highlights that researchers found autonomy was linked with overall wellbeing in the USA, western Europe and beyond.

Mastery: Pink explains this is the desire, opportunity and intent to develop personal skill and ability. Mastery has three laws which are mindset, pain and asymptote. Mindset quite simply is the belief that one can continually get better in spite of any obstacles. Pain is the understanding that in order to significantly improve the performance of ourselves, or the team we are a part of, we will be required to give substantial effort and sacrifice. Finally, asymptote is a personal vision of a target which will always be just out of reach. The player or the colleague has an expectation of themselves which is so high that it will always be just out of reach. However, rather than this being demoralising it has precisely the opposite effect.

Purpose: This has been covered extensively in a team sense but this sense of purpose is individual. It is the cause

of the individual or their *raison d'être*. For some it will be
fulfilling the expectations of parents, supporting one's family,
for others it will be social status and there are a myriad of
other purpose drivers. Whatever the root cause, footballers, policemen, teachers, officer workers are all inherently
looking for affirmation. Where this sense of affirmation arises
from is bespoke. When a manager is looking to address the
issue of an individual's fluctuating motivation, it can be the
key to unlocking this third pillar.

Ole Gunnar Solskjær and Mick Phelan had this concept
well in hand as they had brought together the collective
talents of the Manchester United coaching and support staff.
'We realise we don't have all the answers. Our attitude is
simply to give people what they need to be great at their
jobs. The challenge here is that everyone wants to be the
very best in their field but they can lose focus on being
part of a whole team that gets results on the pitch. That's
the problem with departments. They have walls and walls
divide people,' explained Mick Phelan. I talked to Ole and
Mick about Pink's concepts of motivation. They had not
read his work but their emotional intelligence, experience
and personal character meant that they naturally adopted
the same principles.

Getting the right people on the bus facing the right way

At St Bede's, I have employed a specific model to assess
where the staff body are at in terms of the developments I
set to work on during my first days and weeks. I did this by
establishing who was where in terms of alignment with the

vision and direction. It is a model created by Swedish writer and psychologist, Claes Janssen. Janssen has developed an internationally respected theory which identifies the states individuals can be in during any transition, such as the first 100 days of a new manager's reign.

As Janssen describes on his website: 'In all change, we move from a Contentment, which is lost, via a period in Denial, which is a defence of the old, through Confusion, which ends when we give up whatever it is of the old that had to be given up. The giving up is the turning point, making us open to the possibilities, the new, whereby we move on to Renewal.' The 'Rooms of Change' model highlights the flow of psychological movement during a transitional period.

Janssen's Rooms of Change Model

Any football team, office or organisation will have those who are in a state of contentment with the status quo. Once a new leadership comes along and shares a new vision, a script and an implementation plan, there can often be a state of denial. This state can be challenging, aggressive and perhaps at worst, apathetic. Individuals in this state can look for allies, those who may hold onto the belief that this is just another transition which will come and go, at which time the existing state of affairs will resume.

When transitional arrangements do begin to take shape, visions turn to concrete action and visible change can be seen, states of confusion can be created with those who are unsure whether to join the early adopters or cling to their denial.

Finally, for those who manage to stay the course or are immediately desperate for a change, there is the state of renewal. This state is often seen on the pitch following a change in manager. The impact of a new manager, leader or CEO can be akin to a spiritual enlightenment. There can be visible signs of increased energy, belief and cohesion. There are countless examples of a change in manager resulting in, at least in the short-term, an improvement in a team's results. There is an apparent rejuvenation amongst the players, the supporters and everyone connected.

More often the challenge of change can be littered with challenges of denial and confusion before the state of renewal is achieved. With the first 100 days, it is imperative that denial and confusion are dealt with by winning by hearts and minds. Winning hearts entails the sharing of a compelling vision alongside quickly developed relationships. Winning minds is achieved through a clear understanding of the rewards and consequences of not adopting the change.

Day 18 – 'We' and 'Our'

In order to get the views of the staff, I asked our new union representatives to carry out a survey to gather the thoughts of staff around what was working in general and what we could improve. I then asked them to detail an agenda that we could discuss in order to make some improvements to improve our efficiency.

The confidence to do this again came from the discussion over another curry with Micky. We shared ideas around getting the inside information as to what our teams were thinking. It boiled down to simply asking them. Perhaps I had expected Micky to be more authoritarian but I was again impressed and in awe of his emotional intelligence. He explained how he asked his captain regularly for support in understanding the mood of the group.

'While I don't always follow up on what they might want,' he explained, 'I at least act in a way that is conscious of their thoughts about the way things are going.'

On Day 18, the results of our staff survey were presented to me by our union reps. They had highlighted three priorities which they believed were the three key issues. We did not just discuss the problem in our meeting that morning, we also discussed possible solutions. I was really impressed by their understanding of the whole school's need to improve and drive towards our vision. They were very much on board the bus and now we were all discussing the best route to take in order to get to our agreed destination. The meeting closed with some actions and a time to come back and review our progress. The key words here are 'We' and 'Our'. In our early conversations, Micky would strongly challenge me if I used 'I' or 'My'. 'It's all about the team. Never forget that,' he said on more than one occasion. From that staff voice, our teaching team became much more cohesive, united behind the reality that we had the vast majority of our team players on the bus, facing the right way and feeling a part of our journey together.

Team talks for change

Once you have established who is where in the rooms of change in your organisation it is time to lead the change that you need to see. When Micky took over at Tranmere Rovers, he quickly set about highlighting the need for change, working through it step by step. 'We needed to get the urgency of the situation into the players' heads. I stopped training during the first session I took and I laid into the players about their lack of intensity. I told them a few home truths about the expectations on them as players and what they needed to be doing if they ever wanted to play at a higher level.

'Then I started to get those experienced pros, some of them I'd won promotion with before, to start hammering home our standards and the expectations on you as a player for this club. I was building that coalition with key voices that I knew would keep the key messages going even when I wasn't there. Like I said earlier, I spoke to the group about treating them like the champions they wanted to be. I was getting that buy-in from an ambitious group of lads. We got those quick wins all over the place and then, as we always do as a coaching team ... we never let up. We focus on every day, every training session being better than the last.'

The need for change can come to even the strongest teams, especially in sport. The change model is described by John Kotter, the best-selling business author and Professor of Leadership, Emeritus at Harvard Business School, in his book 'Leading Change'.

Kotter's model is a process which is frequently followed by the most successful football managers either consciously or unconsciously. Reassuringly, the process is transferable and will allow leaders to support members of the team or company through the rooms of change in order that renewal can be achieved.

Kotter's eight-step model for change

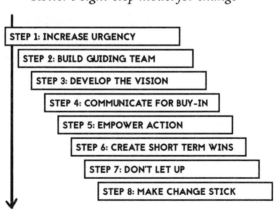

This model of change is transferable to business and education. At St Bede's, we needed to change a culture of top-down management Over time, there had become entrenched views that senior leaders had the solutions, or at least should do, and the middle leaders work largely to improve their own area but not the whole school performance. In order to change this culture, I was able to state the need for urgent change through whole staff meetings, middle leaders' meetings and individual conversations. A coalition of support was sought through conversations I had with people who I saw at both middle and senior level that could bridge this leadership divide. After discussing this with leaders across the school, the need and desire for urgent change was established. Quite simply, unless leaders worked more cohesively then the potential of the school to improve was limited.

The most important stage in this change process was the empowering of colleagues. Middle leaders were given roles of responsibility that allowed them to act as a voice for the entire staff body. Whether these roles were union roles or whole school leadership roles, they opened up a flow of communication that the staff felt built trust and cohesion. In our Ofsted inspection, I was delighted to hear that this was reflected in middle leader interviews with our inspectors.

In Kotter's eight-step model, the first three steps detail the formation of reason, gathering of a coalition and method of delivery. Effectively, this is the preparatory work which offers the most change for effective communication followed by an engagement motivated by a shared understanding of the future. The final three steps are short, medium and long-term actions that maintain the momentum from the transition. All of the actions taken along this eight-step model must be taken in the context of the knowledge already established from the work completed in the first four chapters of this book. Short-term wins, though, must be effective early in the 100-day process. Micky was keen to stress: 'While there will be no guarantees, especially in the world of professional football management, following a process like this with the correct prior knowledge gives the manager the best chance of success in leading change. You've just to make sure that you're making these decisions with a knowledge of people, their motivations and their role in the steps needed for winning change. If you've got the right coaching staff and you're using the right approach to winning games, you give yourself a chance of getting people aligned and then winning games of football, increasing your sales or improving your company's performance.'

Reflections

1. How will you create the opportunities to really get to know your team?

2. Who will your captains be?

3. How will you ensure that these captains are constantly referred to?

4. What are the key characteristics of the people you need on your bus?

5. How will you identify who has what is required and who does not?

6. What are the key changes you will make?

7. How will you go about doing this?

8. *How will you create space for your team to grow?*

9. *What change model/steps will you take to give yourself the best chance of leading change?*

10. *Can the rooms of change be applied in your change management?*

11. *What will your action plan look like in order to affect the change you want to see?*

12. *Putting all that together, what are your three priorities to increase the effectiveness of your team?*

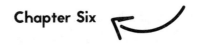
DAY 20-35

 Kaizen cultures: Tearing down the walls and welcoming the world

Cultural revolution at Carrington

As the wins continued to roll in, Ole Gunnar Solskjær and Mick Phelan were gaining traction. They saw that the impetus was with them and that the culture of the club was beginning to slowly turn. As they grew familiar with their old surroundings at Carrington, they began to see the ways in which they believed they could rekindle the culture that they had experienced during the reign of Sir Alex Ferguson. The pair began to make the changes to keep the longer-term cultural change moving, they created a Kaizen culture by redesigning the departmental geography of the training ground and welcoming external expertise. 'We felt the change we wanted to make with this place was departments,' explained Mick Phelan. 'There were walls that were dividing people and we wanted to bring people together,' he continued.

Beginning with the departmental redesign, Ole explained: 'When we arrived, the coaching staff were spread around the place. The youth coaches were on the other side of the bridge and we might not see them during the day. We wanted them to be a part of what we were doing so that we had a coaching team right through the age groups.'

'It didn't sit right with me that we had the player liaison people next to our office here and the youth coaches on the other side of the training ground,' added Mick. 'So we moved the player liaison staff over to the other side of the car park (on the opposite side the training ground) and brought the whole coaching staff over here. We wanted all the football side of things to be together. My attitude was that it should be the players who go looking for their liaison workers and not the other way around.' If they could not do it physically, the managerial pair were metaphorically tearing down the walls at the Carrington training ground.

As well as the internal developments, Ole and Mick were determined to draw on the links to club had in order to bring in fresh ideas. Micky and I asked Mick and Ole about how they were looking to develop a Kaizen culture. Though the language may have been unfamiliar, they were familiar with the Japanese concept of continuous improvement throughout the organisation. Mick, in particular, wanted to shift United to be an outward-facing organisation.

'At United, we used to be the people that everyone came to. They wanted to see how we won and what we did. We probably – the club, that is – got a bit complacent and stopped looking on the outside. We know we can always get better and we'll speak to whoever we think can help us.'

It was clear that this inner confidence was born from a comfortable vulnerability that really epitomised the humility and modesty of the pair. These qualities are the reason that both Ole and Mick brought smiles to the faces of those at Carrington and Old Trafford during their first 100 days. Quietly, Ole and Mick had created an evolving culture which was true to the traditions of United. They were creating a cultural revolution which was bringing together a family that had lost its way, just as much as they were turning the team around the pitch.

Kaizen is King – inside the room of truth

Following a presentation titled: *'If Toyota was a football club, what would it look like?'*, Micky received a standing ovation following a presentation to fellow managers on his UEFA Pro Licence course. He highlighted that the top managers leading the top teams drive a culture which encourages players, staff and managers to look at the standard activities which take place every day at the football club. This may include the food eaten at lunch, the timings of training sessions, the technology used to analyse performance and the fitness regimes that are employed.

All of these areas of team development can be standardised week on week. However, they are not standardised and then simply accepted. Micky encourages his coaching staff and players to feed back how they believe small, incremental changes can be made to improve the process in order to reach the desired outcome. Micky and his coaching staff will reflect on these processes regularly in order to employ the principle of Hansei. Managers and coaches around the world are famed or revered for the great leaps of innovation but it is the culture of Kaizen through Hansei which leads to a learning organisation which can continuously improve.

Enhancing a culture through language and some early wins is a positive start to the first 100 days. Beyond those early successes, Micky ascribes to the Toyota model for continuous improvement. 'With a Kaizen culture, you drum into everyone that we are looking to continually improve. We'll be looking for the small margins that will give us an edge. That has to run right the way through the team. Our physio, our fitness coach and everyone else is looking for the small gains. We have that mentality every day in the way that we train and prepare. For example, we look at the GPS to see how far the players are running. The more we analyse, the more we can tailor training to individual players. Kaizen cultures also consider input from external sources. It's that idea of Hansei, that we always believe we can better and we can improve what we do by looking at it in a different way. At Dundee United, we've had a sports psychologist, Dr Gill Cook from Liverpool John Moores University, working with the players and the staff. At Tranmere, we had Leroy, the chef in the training ground kitchen, and we talk with him about the best foods before and after training. When you've got everyone looking for the marginal gains, you've got a Kaizen culture. A culture like that is only going to help the team continuously improve over the course of the year.'

During a visit to the club's training ground, Micky and I spent time in the 'Room of Truth'. The room itself looks like a classroom and it is the room where no words are left unspoken and everyone gets to voice their opinion on what is going well and what is not. 'You've got to have a room of truth in a Kaizen culture. It's where we very deliberately practise our constant reflection and deep analysis,' explains Micky. 'In our room of truth we comb over the previous games and we point things out that we need to do better. Even if we've won, perhaps even more importantly if we've won, we look at the things that we must do better if we're going to keep improving. The players know that they can say anything in there because you've got to have the honesty if you're going to improve as a group. When you've got your team demanding nothing but the best from each other, respectfully of course, then you've got a Kaizen culture that gives you a great chance of winning football matches.' This 'truth finding' is all about reflection, consultation and improvement which is a process the Japanese refer to as Hansei.

Making marginal gains through Hansei and Kaizen is not limited to business and sport. There are also many examples in schools that are high performing and constantly evolving. Earlier in this book, we looked at Olympic rowing champion and author, Ben Hunt-Davis. 'Will It Make The Boat Go Faster?' described Hansei and Kaizen as being process-driven. He is clear that in order to make teams successful and sustain that success, 'Don't focus on the result; focus on the process that will get you the results.'

Hunt-Davis found that crews were unsuccessful in winning gold because they were solely focused on winning that medal without truly considering the process. He uses the analogy of a cooking recipe. While exploring this analogy he explains that you might get lucky with ingredients and measurements but it will then be difficult to recreate. In effect, there needs to be a standardisation of process and then a desire to 'get curious about the recipe'. While other teams judged success in terms of winning regattas, Hunt-Davis judged success on specific variables such as agendas in meetings, time-keeping, listening along to the speed of the oar. Hunt-Davis goes on to relate such a process focus to people in the world of business who look at the end destination rather than the steps needed to get there. He suggests that our most powerful tool for improvement is attention. That is, attention to the details which make up the result, the end product or the outcomes. A win in football can occur from a fluke decision, an opponent's poor performance or a moment of individual brilliance. A great innovation can occur from a moment of creativity or a chance encounter. In order for success to be maintained, it is crucial to be process-driven, constantly looking to learn from Hansei and Kaizen.

Leaders can operate cultures based upon Hansei and Kaizen by analysing the standard operations across the organisation. This analysis should then include Hansei, reflection and then lead to Kaizen, improvement. The King Kaizen Model (right) is a simple tool which could be used to support the employment of the two fundamentals to a learning organisation where Kaizen becomes king.

In the example shown on the opposite page, the standard operations relate to a football training session as the specific variable, however, there is a clear parallel to leaders of any regard.

King Kaizen Model

Standard Operation	Reflection (Hansei)	Improvement (Kaizen)
Evaluated Outcome		
Timings of the session		
Player understanding		
Player exertion		
Equipment preparation		
Player feedback		
Post-session warmdown		
Coaching staff feedback		

Creating a Kaizen culture

As I got to Day 20, I really wanted our initial pacey improvements to take hold across the school. Top managers use the initial wins and momentum to give reinforced confidence amongst the players and the fans. They do this by creating a culture of continuous improvement. I needed to make sure that my leadership and the leadership of my team supported this. Micky and I set about discussing just how a culture of continuous improvement can be created.

'In every organisation you can be sure of one thing, there will be a culture,' Micky told me. 'The culture may be one that exudes success, high expectations and positive alignment towards a common goal. However, for most football managers, or new leaders of any description, that is not the environment that they inherit when they first walk in the building.' For the football manager, such a utopian environment is highly unlikely due to the nature of most managerial appointments. Most positions become vacant because the previous incumbent has failed to live up to the expectations of the owners, players and supporters. As Sam Allardyce explains: 'More often than not you're walking into a dysfunctional situation. You're often hit by a culture that has led to poor performances and bad results.'

Alternatively, the former manager may have exceeded expectations and moved on to progress their career at a higher level, although it is rare in football. In other leadership posts, however, this is more likely. This can also create challenges. For example, I had taken on my head-teacher post following the previous head's successful six-year tenure. Rather than a sense of despondency and failure, I walked into a culture that had seen outcomes increase, budgets grow and buildings improve under the steward-ship of the former headteacher and the current business manager, Annette Southworth.

Day 21 – Tackling a dysfunctional leadership team

After just over four weeks, one of the members of my leadership team at St Bede's remarked: 'We (the senior leadership team) are like a group of family members who didn't really get on but had to come together at Christmas time. We're a bit dysfunctional. That really needs to change if we're going to get this school to the place that we know it can get to.' I listened intently to my colleague. I'd known that his words were true from the first day I had walked into the school but I hadn't quite managed to put my finger on why that was. There was a fear amongst the team. A fear that seemed to grip them to the point that they feared making a mistake so much that they would not take risks and their creative energy was being held back.

There was no doubt they were committed to the cause and determined to be successful but it became clear on this day that the dysfunctional nature of the team could be a limiting factor moving forward. One thing that had always struck me about Micky and his backroom staff is that they were so aligned. They seemed to work together seamlessly. If Micky was not in the room, they would know what he would think and what he would expect of them. He seemed to have instilled in them a collective drive. He clearly had really high expectations of them but they did not seem to act in a way that was controlled by fear of failure. Instead, they seemed inspired by him and there was a great trust amongst them.

When Micky and I met, it would usually be with Andy Hodgen. Andy is the Head of Sports Science. He was close to the age of the players and worked with them on the ground. He had to push them physically in the gym and on the training ground along with pre and post-match sessions on game days. Andy epitomised the work ethic and standards in Micky's backroom team. He knew the high expectations and the accountability of this role but he acted with the knowledge of Micky's support and his backing in tough conversations with players. I saw this first hand as the three of us ate dinner at an Argentinian steakhouse.

That night we enjoyed a great steak along with some Chilean red wine. During the evening, Micky described an event that day when he made his frustrations known to his backroom team. Micky had taken a player to task over what he saw as a lack of effort during the training session that day. 'I pulled him to one side and said, 'You're not giving me everything today. You know what our standards are here. What's going on today?' Then the player told me, 'I'm injured gaffer. I've told Hodge (Andy) and the other coaches. They told me to just take it easy so I'm ready for the match at the weekend.' So I was stood there feeling a bit daft. I was frustrated with the coaches because they should have told me. I should know that. They know that I should know that. So we'd dropped below our levels of communication. I pulled Hodge and the other lads to one side and said we can't have that happening. Didn't I Hodge!' Micky turned to Andy who nodded. 'Your players or your staff have got to see a united front from their leaders though. I'd never let them (the players) know I was disappointed in that moment with our coaching team.' It was clear from this Micky showed trust and respect in his leadership team but he held them to the highest standards. They knew the levels that are expected of them every single day but they also know the manager had their back.

I remembered this when I started to unpick why our leadership team was dysfunctional. I spoke to Micky on the night of Day 21. He was driving back from scouting a youth game in Southport. We talked through this culture of fear. 'You need to show them that you trust them. They need to be clear on what your expectations are. Get your systems in place to do that and agree with them what principles you should be working to. Then hold them to that. Then you get rid of any lack of clarity. They can then feel safe because that's really important. You've got to make the people you're leading feel safe, challenged and pushed but safe.'

The next day, Day 22, I set about meeting with my leadership team. I discussed their roles again with them individually. We went back over what would make them successful in their roles and how this would benefit the school. Then, the next time we met, a couple of days later, I said explicitly what I'd seen in a leadership team meeting. It was like a weight being lifted from them. They said they had felt fear of making mistakes. We discussed how we would deal with mistakes in the future. This involved being honest about it, understanding that as individuals and a group we would make mistakes but once we had made them once, we would work on what to do so it did not happen again.

It worked well, almost immediately. Our senior leader for analysing data spoke about our current system not being systematic or forensic enough. This led to a conversation about what we could do to improve it. There was a lot more honesty. It also improved relationships around our leadership table. There was less tension and defensive language.

This is still evolving even well beyond the 100 days. Such a change in behaviours of the leaders is a culture shift which requires time and reassurance. Trust is then developed gradually over time.

Sam sings the Blues – the 'Zone of Operation'

Sam Allardyce was a player in an era when Everton Football Club were a dominant force in English football. Allardyce explained to Micky: 'Many people believe that, had English teams not been banned from European competitions in the mid-1980s, Everton could have been crowned European champions. I saw Everton play with a particular style that saw them achieve great success. The style was direct, moving the ball quickly from the defence to the forwards with quality and as a few passes as possible. This is a common strategy in football but it is a strategy that has perhaps become unfashionable in the modern game.'

When Allardyce took up the role as manager at Everton he noted a gap in the perception of the football culture and the reality. He explained: 'The perception was that Everton played the game in a very different way to that of their glory years. The perception was that they followed the model of teams like Barcelona, Real Madrid or even Manchester City. This perception involved a style of play which saw the ball moved quickly on the ground with the goal being to dominate possession and win matches through the technical ability of the players. Playing with the flair of one of Europe's elite is really hard to do. If it wasn't hard to do then everyone would be doing it.'

Allardyce would say that playing the ball 'out from the back' would be his preferred style of play. However, there is often a gap between the realistic ability of the players to play in this way and the expectations of the supporters. This became a problem as the approach of Allardyce, which was ultimately successful in taking Everton away from the relegation zone, was at odds with the perceived culture of the club amongst the fans and pundits. In discussion with Micky, Sam was clear that in order to create a desired culture in a club, you must first understand the perceived culture. 'You've got to recognise what the fans and the pundits are expecting to see. Then, in some form, you've got to explain how you're delivering that. I've had experiences of the 'West Ham Way', the 'School of Science' and the 'Everton Way'. You've got to understand the culture of the place and deliver your messages to the board, the supporters and the media with this in mind.'

Day 25-28 – talk to people, get the full picture

As a headteacher, it is crucial to create a curriculum which meets the needs of the students. The education a school offers the students, both inside and outside the classroom, has to consider the local, national and international environment those children will grow into. Just as Micky and Sam explained how they adapted their approach according to the circumstances, so I began analysing our school context in detail on Day 25.

I met with the primary headteachers whose students made up the majority of our intake. They told me much about the education they offered, the expectations of their parents and the contextual challenges they faced. On Day 26, I met with our career adviser who told me all about the futures our students moved on to. The detail of this added to my understanding of where our students came from, as now I got a picture of where they were going. On Day 27 and 28, I met college principals and vice-principals who spoke to me in great detail about the ways they believed they could support us in preparing our students for further education. They also briefed me on the strengths and weaknesses students from St Bede's arrived at college with.

This was important in showing me my own 'Zone of Operation'. The decisions I now made on medium and longer-term planning could be made in the context of this broader understanding. I was using the crest of the wave, which Sam described to Micky and I, to make connections and quick changes that could support longer-term development. Beyond Day 28, I asked our Senior Assistant Head to go and speak to the students from St Bede's who were now at college. They gave a really interesting insight in to how we had prepared them for the next step. We also asked our new students how they felt after settling into school. There's only one way to understand your zone of operation, that is to talk to people who represent all points of view. Once you have that understanding, decisions are more likely to be successful for medium and longer-term development.

Leaders must clarify their zone of operation. That is, what is the perceived culture, what is the reality of the situation and what must the leader do in order to be successful within the parameters? Richard Barrett, globally renowned leadership author and consultant, has studied organisational values extensively. Barrett's consultancy firm even offer a service which maps organisational cultures. In his book, 'Building a Values-Driven Organisation', Barrett details how leaders can understand and affect the cultural identity of the organisation. For a football manager or business leader, getting to grips quickly with cultural values maps out the emotional and historic factors at play within those first 100 days and beyond.

Once the cultural values are established then the methods of communication, the messages and the mantras that are shared can be tailored. The tailoring of this communication must play on the perceived culture and reassure members of the organisation that this culture is valued. However, within the zone of operation changes can be made, often rapidly, but under the umbrella of the pre-existing cultural expectations. If we think of the STARS model, then such an approach is crucial when we are working within an organisation that requires accelerated growth, realignment or sustaining success. Where the culture is either non-existent, as in a start-up or turnaround situation, then the zone of operation is much wider and members of the organisation are likely to be much more receptive and accepting of swift cultural change.

Tuesday Humby was able to quickly rip up the existing culture of working habits due to the fact that it was clearly broken. However, following public meetings centred on the academisation of the existing school, one word did strike a chord which she was able to use to her advantage.

The parents were fervently opposed to the change of the school name and, as they perceived, the academy chain taking away a beacon of the community. They used the word 'loyalty' to the previous school repeatedly.

In the subsequent 100 days following Tuesday's appointment, she referred to this loyalty as part of an ongoing mantra to reinforce the fact that the school was still their community school and they could still feel loyalty towards it. The community of students, staff and parents then felt a sense that the school was still 'theirs' and that the swift cultural changes that were taking place were cognizant of the past while being driven toward the future. The zone of operation was broad though as the staff were fully aware that the current state of affairs, which included an Ofsted grading of inadequate, would cost the school its future and their jobs if it was not turned around.

Defining the Zone of Operation

EXISTING CULTURE	● What do the internal and external stakeholders believe the exisiting culture of the organisation is? ● What aspects of the existing culture do they believe are positive and which are negative?
CULTURE REQUIRED	● What is the optimum culture required in order to achieve the negotiated success? ● How far is the existing culture away from this and in what ways?
ACTIONS REQUIRED	● What operations are required within the zone of operation in order to achieve this cultural change? ● What are the key messages that both harness the pride from the past and talk of a better future?
METHODS OF COMMUNICATION	● How will the language of the past be weaved with a future vision? ● What methods can be used to evaluate the cultural changes that have been achieved?
FORMS OF EVALUATION	● How will the impact of the changes within the zone of operation be made? ● What methods can be used to evaluate the cultural changes that have been achieved?

Fighting fear

'Fear is the biggest danger for any footballer,' said Sam Allardyce when asked about player mentality. 'I believe that motivation is not the key emotional and psychological aspect that must be addressed but rather the sense of fear. Fear can be paralysing and it can lead to players capitulating under the pressure of the big games. The thing with fear is that it can run right through a team and you've got to be wary of it. There is no hiding place from mistakes and errors on a football pitch with the voice of a thousand judgemental and emotional-charged individuals ready to shout their opinions at young players who can be really affected by it.'

Micky spoke to me about the ways in which he tries to counter fear. 'You've got to think about who you're speaking with. I try to remind myself why I'm there and in situations where someone has made a mistake, I'm there to try to make sure that it doesn't happen again and that the player knows how they can improve. The majority of the time, you don't need to point out mistakes because they know they've made them. Leadership is not about humiliating people, it's about empowering people to learn from their mistakes.'

While there may not be tens of thousands of supporters judging our performance, it is very possible for people to be frozen by fear in all walks of life.

Often, this fear is driven by organisational cultures which purport to 'name and shame' underperforming colleagues. In education, there are often stories of headteachers and leadership teams that lead through a culture of bullying and intimidation.

Such approaches to leading teams is not sustainable if long-term goals are to be achieved. Furthermore, cultures that rely on harsh systems of accountability and appraisal can reduce the discretional effort given by team members. Often, members of a team will go into survival mode, which leads to behaviours that hide mistakes rather than exploring the reason for them and then working collaboratively to find effective solutions.

In 'Black Box Thinking', Matthew Syed explores organisations, institutions and industries that propagate cultures of fear through a culture of blame.

Syed points to the fact that it is an aspect of human nature that we look to blame someone when there is a disaster or seismic event that leads to an undesirable outcome. He compares the cultures of the medical profession and the airline industry in their contrasting approaches to disaster response and specifically cites examples of medical errors that are not reflected upon in enough detail to prompt effective change so that the mistake is avoided again. In contrast, the information contained within the black box, a recording device which can survive an airline disaster, is analysed forensically in order that there is no repeat. Surgeons or doctors, in contrast, fear being vilified or made a scapegoat should they be seen to make an error that leads to significant harm or death.

Sam Allardyce is a manager that has taken criticism from the media, supporters and even directors for his belief that struggling sides need a break from the pressure of top-flight football much more than those who are being successful.

Allardyce strongly advocates the winter break in order to refresh and recharge players both mentally and physically. In order to achieve this, he often takes his teams to Dubai training camps.

This has become a common practice but one which has been much maligned should the team in question be struggling. It's a criticism that Allardyce disputes.

'When a team is struggling they are under great pressure and they are constantly in the headlines. Going to Dubai gives them the mental and physical break they need. It helps them to start thinking clearly again away from all the pressure of the media and the supporters,' he explained. This is a key strategy used by Allardyce to break away from the paralysing grip of fear that was described earlier in this chapter.

Of course, in most walks of life, January breaks to Dubai are unrealistic.

However, breaking the fear-blame loop is possible in different ways. There must be a transition that involves trust, responsibility and accountability. That is to say that effective teams trust each other and feel responsible to one another. They feel morally obliged to sacrifice their own self-interests for the sake of the team. In order to maintain the structure for trust and responsibility to exist effectively, there must be accountability.

It is the accountability which offers the measure of success that is the guiding light for the team's operations. For the football manager the ultimate accountability measure is the results on the pitch.

The ART Loop

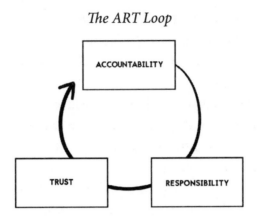

The ball will get turned over – mistakes happen

This model of leadership is one that I have employed at St Bede's during my first 100 days in order to set clear expectations within a positive and productive environment. Accountability in a school setting relates to the educational outcomes of the students. Therefore, clear targets are set based on the students' starting points and ambitious projections. The method of monitoring, reviewing and evaluating the steps being taken to achieve these goals are systematic and transparent. They are also very much based on the notion that it is our responsibility to do our best to improve for our mutual benefit.

Our colleagues are then trusted to implement their own strategies within the school-wide approach to improving school productivity. The ART loop has led to improved outcomes and positive feedback from the staff representatives that are in place to be the mouth piece for all members of the school.

In order for the ART loop to be effective, it must be based upon trust and responsibility. Any time these underpinning features are threatened by individuals tempted to undermine this approach then reminders of accountability can be used through conversations or a re-clarification of expectations. In terms of fear reduction, as made clear in Syed's book, there must be opportunities as part of trust and responsibility, to admit to mistakes and be open about problems.

Such a transparency allows for organisational progression built upon learning. To use the football analogy, there are on average 400 times in a Premier League game that the ball is turned over. As Sam Allardyce points out, this then becomes a crucial factor in the outcome. Making mistakes will be frequent and so it is important to learn from mistakes and not become gripped by the fear of making them. Coaches will always be impressed by the player who never 'hides' after he makes a mistake. They are the players who have the mental resilience to overcome fear of failure. In any organisation, colleagues must be trusted by the manager, CEO or owner to make mistakes but learn from them. Through this, it is possible to build a trusting professional relationship that can help teams grow and perform well in the first 100 days and beyond.

Business as usual (BAU) vs Profit Improvement Plan (PIP)

In order to bring the clarity of expectation to the teams he leads in the first 100 days and beyond, Mark Palios uses timelines. 'I ask the organisations I enter into to produce timelines. If they're seasonal, like retail, these can be on a calendar. So, for example, I will sit with the management team and go through each period to establish Business As Usual (BAU). We have Christmas, then buying in March/April, followed by summer marketing and eventually back to Christmas. Then I ask them to look at that calendar and produce profit improvement plans (PIPs).' The process promotes a Kaizen Culture as it sets out a clear, coherent schedule to improve upon 'business as usual'.

'Initially they'll put all of the PIP actions in the first couple of months but then I'll say 'you can't do this because it's too much, too soon'. Immediately you are building relationships by telling them they can spread out the tasks. PIPs take time and you can't ignore the BAU because it still needs to be done,' Palios explained. 'Again, the first 100 days is about establishing credibility because you need to be sensible about the PIP while maintaining BAU. It's the wrong thing to make big statements without fully understanding both the BAU and the PIP, especially if you're coming into a 'distress' situation. You also need to gain credibility externally, so people put more money in.' There is a clear, calm but relentless approach that Palios exudes which explains his status as a national leader in business turnarounds.

Palios shared one such example of using the improving BAU and PIP process to increase external credibility. He explained: 'One of my biggest successes was persuading money to be invested into a deinking plant in France when no-one was investing in deinking plants. I did this by establishing a credibility amongst foreign and local investors by developing a relationship with the mayor. I understood the currency because of the importance of the mayor. Credibility is the one thing you fight for.'

As Tranmere Rovers struggled in League One at the time of our meeting, Palios stressed the importance of the club's communications team. 'This external credibility gives time to the manager, such as last season when we had injuries and the need for reinforcements. I had a bank of pieces to send out to the press. This created a narrative that could maintain credibility and manage expectations. We now have created breathing space for the players and the managers to develop.'

Palios is clearly focused on the end goal at all times and does not waiver in his approach. His confidence and clarity in the systems he has established creates a solid foundation of internal and external credibility which is crucial for the forging of an ambitious culture based on positive, professional relationships. I witnessed this first hand, observing the relationship between the chairman (Mark Palios) and his manager (Micky). There was clearly a mutual understanding and respect. One statement on the chairman's large mounted board illustrated this perfectly: *The institution not the individual.* Both men were united by a common cause. When any leader can establish this within the first 100 days, the potential for making progress is great.

'Any disasters yet? You're in for a surprise soon'

After the first five weeks as headteacher, Micky visited St Bede's. We sat in my office after a busy day. Micky had a wander around and soaked in the environment. 'So you're enjoying it. Any dugout disasters yet?' he asked. I gave a puzzled luck, to which he responded with a hearty laugh. 'If you've not had one yet then you're in for a surprise soon.' I was still baffled but he reminded me of that relationship analogy he talked to me about in of our first meetings in an Italian fish restaurant. 'You've not had your first argument yet. You've not really said anything that you regret or if not regret then something that is taken the wrong way. It'll come. Just be ready for it when it does and remember to stick to your principles.' I didn't have to wait very long to try his advice out.

Reflections

1. How can you make your culture an outward facing one?
2. Is your leadership team working to the same high standards you expect of yourself?
3. What is the perception of the culture in your new team or organisation?
4. How similar is this to the culture you have observed?
5. How does that impact upon your zone of operation?
6. What happens when people make mistakes?
7. What do the people you work with think about fear at work?
8. How can you create a Kaizen culture?
9. What is your BAU and how can you design a PIP?
10. How strong is your ART loop?

Chapter Seven

DAY 36-50

 Avoiding dugout disasters

The court of the football stadium

The manager can cut a lonely figure as he patrols the technical area beside the field of play. Life for the boss can feel like a trial with a jury of thousands and judges sitting in the stands behind ready to hammer the gavel down should evidence point to a guilty verdict. The guilty verdict, a guilt of perceived failure, can be down to spurious evidence based on false expectations, circumstantial challenges or pure bad luck.

Despite the lack of evidential reliability, the verdict can be damning as it is unfounded. In order to be successful in the court of the football stadium, the manager, acting as plaintiff, must rely on a team around him that can support his case. His defence team are his backroom staff while the evidence is all out there on the pitch. This team, the leadership group, must be highly functioning and ready for the battle. They must avoid the common pitfalls which can beset leadership teams in any walk of life.

For the manager, it is this team that sits alongside him in the dugout. In this chapter, we will look at how to avoid dugout disasters. That is, realigning a team around a cause, challenging the dysfunctions, creating captains and establishing a learning process for all that ensures your team learn how to learn. Failure to take these crucial steps, can lead to catastrophic divisions within a team that can de-rail your first 100 days.

Ole's secret diary and Sir Alex's personal message

'Ah yes,' said Ole, 'I've got it here.' Ole had a notebook in his hand with the image of Old Trafford on the cover. 'I made some notes in here,' he continued. 'December 29th we invited Sir Alex into the training ground.'

As we would hear, Ole had kept notes of his first 100 days to help him recall the steps he had taken to bring change to this grand old club. 'I asked him to come in and speak to the players but he said he didn't want to intrude as they were my team now. When he arrived he said he'd been up all night thinking of what to say to me! He didn't want to speak to the players but he asked to speak to the staff.

'We wanted him back in the club because it's his club! It was also good for the players to see that we weren't afraid of Sir Alex coming down. We wanted him here. He came to look at training and you could see all the players saying, 'it's Sir Alex.' For Ole and Mick, this was all about bringing the identity back to the club and reminding the players about this club's glorious past.'

They also brought in former players to talk to the current team about what it meant to be a United player. 'Roy Keane spoke to the academy players while Darren Fletcher,

Rio (Ferdinand), Vida (Nemanja Vidić), (Dimitar) Berbatov, (Patrice) Evra, just came in to say hi,' Ole explained. 'Everyone talks about tactics nowadays. The gaffer (Sir Alex) doesn't talk about tactics that much, he talks about players. I know him inside out, to a degree.'

Sir Alex had plenty of stories to pass on but he left Ole and his management team with one thought. 'They say all roads lead to Rome. Forget about that, all roads lead to Liverpool. Stop them winning the league! That's what he said,' recalled Ole. Mick and Ole laughed loudly, they knew the value of having Sir Alex in to rekindle that club identity. It was not a particularly calculated move, it just seemed like the obvious thing to do. The managerial duo were indeed recreating the foundations of the United culture. As Mick Phelan was keen to explain, this was an authentic process. 'We weren't particularly overthinking this. It was just an extension of ourselves.'

The key quality in all of these stories is this: authenticity. This is the factor that was quickly building up the credibility of Ole and Mick, not just with the players on the training pitches but amongst the entire staff, community and even the city of Manchester.

Day 36 – seeing red and sticking to your principles

As I reached my first half-term, which lasts about 35 days in school or seven weeks, Micky and I met after training one day. At the time it was mid-October and Tranmere's league form had been solid. The team were performing consistently well and Micky was in good spirits. Following a 5-1 win against Crawley, Tranmere were challenging for promotion in League Two. However, social media 'pundits' had been critical of some recent performances which Micky and I discussed. I had also been criticised for a comment I had made about improving standards in the school. Both issues seemed to correlate to me. I wanted to know how managers deal with the constant judgement of those around them, from both inside and outside of the club.

I dare say that any leader has had a similar realisation at some point in their first 100 days. It is the moment when you realise that you are the one making decisions that will be judged by all in the organisation and those outside. These are the decisions which will effectively make or break your leadership tenure. People will either trust or doubt you by the outcome of these decisions. What I was surprised to learn from the top managers, however, was that even these decisions are not taken in the isolated mind of the manager. They are still decisions which, although the leaders as an individual will be held to account by, are arrived at by discussion, consultation and understanding of a wide range of possible outcomes. What defines the leaders here is that it's this pressure that they thrive from and, in a slightly perverse way, it is the danger of failure which fuels their desire to succeed.

'When you drive in that car park in the morning, you've got to love it. You've got to love the responsibility of it and the expectation on you as the manager,' Sam Allardyce explained to Micky. 'You have to love it because if you don't then you won't get through the tough times.'

Micky added: 'I look at my job like a conductor, looking out across the pitch like the players are your orchestra, playing your symphony to the crowd. The only difference is that a football crowd will scream what they think about your music and I don't think you get that in a theatre. You have to remember that the conductor doesn't turn around to check with the audience what music to play next or change the tune halfway through because they're not sure about it! As a manager, you've got to be strong in that dugout and be mentally tough. That means sticking to your principles when the chips are down. If you do that, your team feeds off it. I remember the (National League) play-off final game (against Boreham Wood at Wembley in 2018). I could sense the panic from the crowd when we had a man sent off after 54 seconds but we'd practised for this. In the dugout, you've got to hope the players feed off the fans' passion but your decisions can't be swayed because of the guy screaming behind you. A conductor does not turn to the audience when he's conducting the orchestra.'

As a headteacher or leader of any organisation, there will always be pressure for knee-jerk responses to situations. There will always be changes to staff and student behaviours in the normal course of a year. In any leadership role, you are dealing with individuals and individual behaviours can fluctuate.

I learnt from the words of Micky and the interviews with elite managers that principles are key in situations that may prompt reflex actions. Clarity and consistency, akin to a conductor conducting their orchestra, give teams of any sort a sense of calm in the storms that inevitably come along with any leader. The rest of this chapter will dig deep into the logistics of a clear, consistent and cohesive leadership style that avoids dugout disasters.

Dysfunctions of the dugout

Whether it be a manager's backroom team, the senior partners of a legal firm or the senior leadership of a school, there are fundamental behaviours required for functional leadership teams. It is the manager's role to set these behaviours and insist upon them in order to create a highly functioning leadership team and avoid dugout disasters. Micky has a clarity with his team which leads to a highly functioning coaching team wherever he has managed. 'Everyone knows their role but they also know what are collective principles are. We are honest with each other and we're not afraid to disagree if that's required. I want people to feel confident to speak up. Ultimately, picking the team and those decisions have to come from me. We'll often get some great debate though about how we're going to approach a game. I want them to have their say, so that they feel an ownership.'

Micky's approach is very similar to the globally-renowned team functionality model created by Patrick Lencioni. Lencioni is the founder and president of The Table Group. The group specialises in executive team development. Their portfolio of clients includes Fortune 500 companies (a list of 500 of the largest companies in the United States compiled by Forbes magazine every year); universities, high-tech start-ups and others. The author knows what makes leadership teams work, regardless of context. In Lencioni's *New York Times* bestseller, 'The Five Dysfunctions of a Team', he outlines corrosive behaviours which can erode a team's chances of success before a ball has been kicked, a sales call made or a lesson taught.

The first dysfunction of any team is a lack of trust created by an unwillingness to show vulnerability. Such an environment can be created by teams that operate on a culture of blame with individuals concerning themselves with only their own performance rather than the achievements of the collective. Secondly, teams that struggle operate with an artificial harmony which can be the fuel for a passive aggressive fire. This destructive force is borne from a fear of conflict. The lack of trust underpins the fear of conflict as there are fragile relationships which could be destroyed due to the absence of a trusting environment.

The Pyramid of Dysfunction

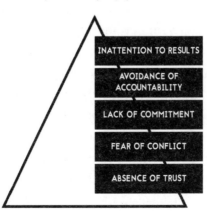

The result of a fear of conflict and the absence of trust makes it unlikely that individuals in the team are willing to commit. As a result, the leadership given by the team can be ambiguous in order that mistakes can be put down to others, misunderstandings or circumstantial factors. There can be an avoidance of accountability, which creates low standards. The rocky ground created means that there is an inattention to results, whether on the training ground, call centre or department. In order to protect the status and ego of the leadership team, the strategies and tactics of the team are not analysed thoroughly.

Sam Allardyce uses the art of visualisation to help create the vision of success. He encourages his players to visualise the game the night before. He encourages them to consider how they will play, how they will react to the opposition and how they will behave when the Premier League drama unfolds. He explains: 'As a manager, you think through what you will do the night before a game. You consider what might happen and how you will react when this happens.

'You give your staff the rundown of your plan in the pre-match conversations and meetings, and push them to chip in or remind you of what your plan was. You want them to make sure you stick to the plan or at least remind you of it in case you miss it in the heat of the moment. It is easier to make these decisions in the dugout then. You can be so focused on the first touch that you can forget sometimes that it's not the first touch that is most important, it's the last.'

Through this process, Allardyce establishes a trust in his team ensuring that his staff challenge him and commit to a solution. Sam pioneered this attention to detail through accountability, stressing that results on the training ground matter as much as on a match day. By encouraging a team of highly analytical staff, Allardyce harnesses their collective talents. This is the essence of a top performing team that is loyal and supportive of an effective leader of the group.

Day 38 – a lesson from Chinese philosophy

'Behaviour is getting better,' I proudly exclaimed in front of the staff at the beginning of Day 38. Whether you teach in an inner-city comprehensive or a leafy independent school, the behaviour and attitudes of students is always a hot topic. I backed the statement up by referring to some key statistics around exclusions and internal incidents. Both figures had come down since the previous year. It was the first time, though, that I would see a collective look of disbelief and almost shock on the faces of our teaching staff during that staff briefing on the morning of Day 38. I immediately realised I was facing my own potential dugout disaster here.

I had clearly misread the mood of our team. It was, then, no surprise to me that the staff representatives asked to speak with me later that day. They came to me at the end of the day to share with me the mood of the staff. The lead representative did not dispute the figures I had shared but pointed out that they did not highlight low-level behaviour, silly interruptions that just slowed learning down. This, it became clear, was a major frustration of the teaching staff which they did not feel was being taken seriously enough by the leadership of the school.

While I was initially frustrated that I had made a sweeping statement and perhaps not considered what the perception of the staff was, I knew that I had unearthed an issue which I could now work with the teaching team to do something about.

That evening, after returning home and lamenting my mistake with my wife over our usual late evening dinner once our three children had been put to bed, I put together various plans for new policies and procedures to help rectify the situation. The next morning, on my commute to work, Micky called and I explained the events of the previous day. I proudly explained my decisive action and how I was going to fix this problem. Micky stopped my flow. 'You're going to face the same problem,' he told me. 'You're trying to fix their problem. Could they come up with their own solution to this behaviour problem?' I immediately dropped my head, sighed and smiled. The answer was obvious: Of course they could. 'You're working in a great school, with strong teachers who are all highly trained and skilled. Don't try to fix their problem, help them to figure it out for themselves. When they come up with the solution, they won't be looking at you when it goes wrong, they'll looking at themselves but crucially they'll really want this to work.'

It was just the advice I needed to hear. In that commute to work, I changed much of my approach and belief systems about leadership. When you are looking to make lasting and real change, people need to feel they have accomplished this, not that it was a leader. I thought back to Micky's interviews, he would never say he had won a game, improved a player or the like. It was always everyone at the club, from the groundsman, to the chairman and the supporters. In the days and weeks following, I followed Micky's advice. We, the whole staff, explored the issues, agreed some simple but significant actions and the result was that, as well as improved statistics, our staff now fed back progress on the behaviour and attitudes of the students. It was a valuable lesson. It is a lesson captured in a quote by Lao Tzu, the ancient Chinese philosopher: 'Go to the people. Live with them. Start with what they know. Build with what they have. So, with the best leaders, when the work is done, the task accomplished, the people will say, 'We have done this ourselves.'' Another lesson on our morning commutes from a football manager to a school headteacher and another twist in this unexpected adventure we were on together…

'Who is your Roy Keane?'

Micky and I discussed the similarities between the dressing room and the staff room. Micky put me on the spot and asked me: 'Who is your Roy Keane?' After initially being confused by the question, Micky then clarified: 'Who is the person that will lead the group when you're not there? Not your assistant or deputy head but your voice in the changing rooms. Who is going to personify the behaviours that you want to see in the building?' While we had four union reps in the school. I knew I needed to further devolve leadership to encourage a shared responsibility and ownership for our collective success as a school.

Perhaps one of Sir Alex Ferguson's most important signings

was a young midfielder from Nottingham Forest who would dominate Premier League games during his illustrious career at Old Trafford. Roy Keane was Ferguson's leader in the dressing room. He set the standards for others to follow and Ferguson knew he had a captain and a leader amongst his team to drive the other players. Keane's reputation went before him and he commanded instant respect. Many managers looked with envy at Ferguson's changing room general. Harry Redknapp was one those managers who focused on Keane's authority amongst his peers as a great strength of Manchester United.

In Redknapp's book 'A Man Walks On To A Pitch,' he questions whether the years that followed Ferguson's departure would have been so fallow had Keane still been in the dressing room. Redknapp explains: 'He (Keane) would have been after them (the players) as he always was in the peak years, when there were no short-cuts at United and those messages were passed on from Sir Alex through Keane. There is a story of him laying into Mark Bosnich, the goalkeeper, for turning up late on his first day of training. Bosnich said he'd got lost. Keane's point was that on his own first day at the club, he got up early, hired a taxi and followed it to the training ground in his car to ensure he arrived on time. He had incredible professional standards and expected the same of everybody. It's great to have a player like that in your team. Every manager wants a Tony Adams, a John Terry or a Roy Keane, a player who will have a go.'

At the beginning of his tenure, England football manager

Gareth Southgate made it very clear that he wished to create a team with devolved leadership. He saw that the English media liked to pin the pressure of team leadership on one player, namely the England captain. After he had dropped the existing captain, Wayne Rooney, Southgate outlined his desire to move away from the 'one captain' leadership model. Rather, Southgate subscribed to the notion that as the manager it was his role to create a team of leaders rather than limit team leadership to one man with an armband.

In a 2017 interview with Sky Sports, Southgate explained more. 'The key for me is how do we develop more leaders? There are moments in a game to go and grab it by the scruff of the neck and moments to step in. But there is nothing to stop other players from doing that. I get the bloke who pulls the armband on for match day is important, but in Euro 96 it was just as important what Stuart Pearce was doing during the week – and Alan Shearer and Teddy Sheringham and Paul Ince – as Tony Adams. In fact, it was David Platt who was captain at the start – Tony took over during the tournament. It is more the culture of the team that is set by the leaders in the group that I think is fundamental to us doing well.'

Southgate, who was initially seen as somewhat of a pioneer with regard to devolved leadership, pointed out that England's most successful team in the last 30 years actually operated a similar model under then manager, Terry Venables. The team, that included Southgate, played with a tenacity and desire driven by a team of leaders. Many of these players go on to captain their club sides and even become managers. It is not coincidence that both the team of Euro 96 that reached the semi-final and the World Cup team of 2018, who also reached the semi-final stage, both had leaders throughout the squad. It is also no coincidence that both Venables and Southgate created leaders not followers.

The world of business has been intrigued by the cultural transformation achieved by Southgate which was so evident in the 2018 FIFA World Cup. In an article in *Business Leader Magazine* titled 'Seven leadership lessons learned from Gareth Southgate,' Sporting Edge director Jeremy Snape praises the manner in which Southgate empowered his team to become leaders in their own right regardless of an armband.

As a director of Sporting Edge – a leading performance consultancy – Snape works with businesses to develop a similar strategy of empowerment. In particular, Snape believes that the one to one work that Southgate carried out proved invaluable in getting to know his squad better.

The repeated cycle of 'Prepare – Do – Review' allows players to self-review and continually improve – a Kaizen culture based upon devolved leadership and a high function-ing team.

Snape explains: 'We can see that even in the big pressure moments like the penalty shoot-out, England backed themselves to win. Business owners and directors can learn a lot from Gareth's leadership approach in dealing with the constant challenge of helping their own teams become high-flyers.'

Day 42 – passing on the school armband

Moving to a school with greater devolved leadership was a key target of mine with my first 100 days. I recognised we needed to get away from a system that was frustrating middle leaders. Middle leaders' meetings, attended by both middle and senior leaders, were led by senior leaders. This had almost become the public platform for middle leaders to vent their frustrations. It was not that anybody had any personal friction but rather the hierarchy that had developed over the years had become beset by frustration on all parts.

On Day 42, I asked to speak with the lead union rep about the issue. He is a long-standing member of staff, the head of the English department with a high level of performance and would be influential amongst colleagues, hence his union position.

I spoke candidly with him about my thoughts on the middle leaders' meetings and what they said about our internal professional relationships. I asked for his views on the matter. He was very clear and honest. In his view, and he represented the views of the many, he felt that it was not a time that was spent productively. He felt more action could be taken in these meetings and we could talk about moving the school forward rather than just passing on information. It was a fascinating insight and one which I was really delighted to hear.

The effect was immediate at the next meeting and the agenda was generated by middle leaders. There was a great ownership and now a realisation that my words earlier in the 100 days would be backed up by action. A key meeting on the calendar was now owned by the people who are the driving force of any school. The middle leadership team at the school are truly exceptional. I encouraged excellent leaders in Maths, PE, Science, RE, History, Geography, Creative Arts and other areas to become what is known as Subject Leaders of Education. This would allow them to share their experience across schools in the region whilst also learning from others. The additional levels of responsibility were intended to reflect my confidence in them and hopefully boost the confidence they had in themselves.

Later in my first year, the middle leaders who were interviewed by our Ofsted inspection team, said that this was a significant improvement in the way the school was being run. We were now looking to improve our school collectively.

At first I was baffled when Micky asked who my captains were. Now I knew who they were very clearly and it was allowing me to think with much more clarity about how we were improving St Bede's together, as a team.

Leaders learn to plan, do and review

A leadership group in any organisation must practise the art of learning. As the first 100 days of a leader's reign progresses, devolved leadership that incorporates collective planning, cohesive action and thorough review can be described as metacognitive learning. Gareth Southgate's approach of 'prepare, do, review' is a very deliberate approach that encourages his players to become leaders of their own learning.

Such an approach can be adopted by any organisation or team in order to create a culture of self-regulated learning. Within this culture, players, students or colleagues, develop a metacognition which gives them the skills to learn how they learn. With this ability an organisation can grow in a sustainable, organic manner. As a result, individuals are empowered and thus develop leadership qualities under-pinned by a conscious confidence.

The use of coaching or teaching styles that encourage metacognition and self-regulated learning are amongst the most effective as highlighted by research conducted by the Education Endowment Fund. The research, which is the driver for much contemporary educational practice in the UK, highlights key recommendation which while predomi-nantly aimed at education professions, can be understood and utilised in any organisation.

As illustrated the table that is featured in the next pages, leaders in any setting can create learning environments with every member of the team becoming a leader of their own learning.

*Leadership of effective
metacognitive and self-regulated
learning environments*

Step 1

Action: Leaders should acquire the professional understanding and skills to develop their teams' metacognitive knowledge.

Example: Gareth Southgate travelled around the globe to see the practices used by various leading sports coaches. In one trip he watched NBA coaches develop setpieces and utilised this preparation to arrange the highly effective England setpieces at the 2018 World Cup.

Intended outcome: Leaders will have the ability to develop systematic processes that allow team members to develop their metacognitive approaches i.e. 'Plan, do, review'.

Step 2

Action: Explicitly teach team metacognitive strategies, including how to plan, monitor and evaluate their learning.

Example: Micky talks of sitting his players down, explaining the style of the opposition and asking them to come up with a tactical approach. Micky then asks the players to evaluate the results of their approach and learn from the experience.

Intended outcome: The process encourages team players to plan a strategy when faced with a clear objective. For example, how to play against a team that plays with three at the back. This creates leadership of the actions from within the group.

Step 3

Action: Model your own thinking to help the team develop their metacognitive and cognitive skills.

Example: Leaders articulate their own approach and explain how this has led to their understanding of the game. Sam Allardyce does this through statistical analysis which is referenced when explaining an approach to his teams.

Intended outcome: Modelling by the leader is a fundamental in order to give clarity to the team around an agreed approach to a metacognitive approach. This offers an 'expert' approach which can be followed by the members of the team.

Step 4

Action: Set an appropriate level of challenge to develop teams' self-regulation and metacognition.

Example: Tuesday Humby set out milestone steps to the ultimate goal of taking the school toward a much improved Ofsted grading. Teachers were then asked to plan together, evaluate their success and enhance the teaching and learning in the classrooms. Thorough analysis and response to self and peer feedback resulted in swift and sustained improvements.

Intended outcome: Challenge is essential to set high standards which stretch the group to believe in something that may seem barely possible. The challenge must be stretching but appropriate, possible and clear in order to enhance performance.

Step 5

Action: Promote and develop metacognitive talk.

Example: Language such as 'Plan, do, review' became part of the England camp. As a result, they looked at every action, performance and every training session with an independence and confidence that allowed for self-regulated learning.

Intended outcome: The use of key languages is crucial in order to create a shared understanding. This allows for guided, purposeful practice that builds upon the team players' prior knowledge.

Step 6

Action: Explicitly teach team members how to organise and effectively manage their learning independently.

Example: Claudio Ranieri taught his Premier League title-winning Leicester City side how to learn independently and manage their own match intelligence. As Jamie Vardy, the team's top goalscorer, described in a 2015 interview: 'Each player has his own camera on him so he can analyse them and see what they're doing. We get to watch them on the iPads all week – we have to make sure we watch them and take it on board.'

Intended outcome: With a process that is systematic, guided and explicitly metacognitive it is possible to give instructions on how to enhance performance through 'plan, do, review' that eventually becomes second nature and engrained into the culture of an organisation.

Leaders who create sustained success need leaders who

lead from within. The ability of members of the team to enhance their own skills and learning is pivotal for this sustainability. Whether it is Gareth Southgate's England squad, Claudio Ranieri's Leicester City, Micky's Dundee United/Tranmere Rovers or Graham Henry's All Blacks, metacognitive skills are crucial for sustained success.

Educational research points to the tremendous impact this has on school children but this impact is also visible amongst teams that incorporate devolved leadership.

Day 49 – planning for the second half

We established a 'plan, do, review' system for the next academic year. I met with Andrew Holt, our Assistant Headteacher, who came to me with an exciting idea for research into metacognition. After a good two-hour discussion, we arrived at 'Learning Power' as an understanding and exciting handle for our plan.

Andrew had worked hard to get an understanding of how many staff were already using an approach that looked to improve the learning power of our students. From this, we discussed how that could be shared across school in order to improve our whole school teaching.

Once again, this was another leader, keen to engage in work that could improve the school. We worked well together. Andrew brought research and a philosophical grounding. I added a systematic approach of how to incorporate 'plan, do and review' into the timetable.

This grew into an action plan which will now be used to improve the teaching at the school over the next year. The focus, like the focus on behaviour improvement, came from the views of the teaching staff who felt our students could be more independent and resilient. Therefore, our work to improve this area was generated from the feedback of our team.

By Day 49, we were now planning for the medium to long-term as the short-term wins had been achieved and there was a real direction to our journey of improvement.

Half-time – finding my voice

At St Bede's, I arrived at the halfway point of my first 100 days in a strong position. It seemed as though the staff were eager to work together to improve the school. We had hit bumps in the road but overcome these and become stronger for it. There was a confidence about the way in which I believe I was acting as a new headteacher and there was positive feedback from all quarters. Like football, though, just when everything seems be running smoothly, when the wins appear to keep coming, the shock of a defeat can be extremely deflating.

We had some disappointing behaviour by a large group of students which I needed to address. I also had a member of staff come to me to describe how they felt unappreciated. I realised that both situations required action in terms of my communication with both staff and students.

While devolved leadership was in full flow, the teaching staff felt represented and heard, a leader was still required to be the figurehead that praised all and acted as a guiding light for vision and ethos.

Micky posed me a question which resonated a great deal over another dinner one Thursday evening in Liverpool. 'What are your team talks like?'

He continued: 'How are you talking to your team about their performance, good and bad. Do they know what you think? Are you improving what they do with the messages you're giving them? How are you constantly reminding them about what you're all there for through your messages?'

The truth was that I was not sure. I did not know and had not really thought about the way I was speaking to our staff and students. Although I had done a lot of work on addressing vision, mission and values, this was not enough to maintain a collective direction throughout the first 100 days. I needed to hear more about when, where and how the most effective team-talks can be given.

As I moved into the second half of my first 100 days – the crucial second 45 minutes when games can be won or lost by a right or wrong decision on the pitch – investigating and delivering match-winning team talks became the starting point for Micky and I.

Reflections

1. How functional is your team's pyramid?

2. How will you create a basis of trust through relationships?

3. Is there safe conflict involving challenge and support?

4. Does your team commit to agreed actions?

5. How clear are your systems of accountability?

6. Is the end result defined and analysed closely?

7. Who are the leaders in your organisation?

8. *How will you stimulate devolved leadership?*
9. *Once devolved, which leaders in your organisation can enhance the growth of the group?*
10. *How will you facilitate systems of effective devolved leadership?*

Chapter Eight

DAY 51-65

 Team talks

'That stays in the dressing room'

After the drama of 45 minutes plus injury time, the football field empties as the 22 players walk down the tunnel and enter the dressing room. As they do so, the thousands of spectators in the stadium and potentially the millions watching around the world imagine the words they would use to propel their team into the second half. During the first 100 days these team talks can play a part in defining the relationship that the players have with the manager. They see how the manager reacts under pressure. They see how he treats a player who has just made a mistake. They see how he addresses underperformance or a lack of attention to the detailed tactical preparations. They see how the manager behaves and they all make a judgement which underpins their trust and sense of belonging.

I knew there was so much to be learnt from managers like Ole Gunnar Solskjær, Sean Dyche and Micky in the area of motivational speaking. In this chapter, we will hear more about that strategies and resilience of these leaders at key times.

In education, there is a great deal written about low morale and a large percentage of teachers leave the profession. There is a wide range of reasons for this such as increasing workloads, poor student behaviour and oppressive leadership systems. While there was a low turnover of staff at St Bede's, I knew the school could fall victim to this. I needed to use my team talks, as well as leadership style, to fight against this and create an optimistic, inspired and fulfilled staff group. My team talks could articulate this and perhaps even cultivate such an atmosphere.

There are many examples of managers who have failed to inspire and lead through their team talks. It is an issue recognised by European football's governing body, UEFA, in the leadership courses they deliver. UEFA's Pro-Licence course has been obligatory for top-flight managers since 2003. One of the UEFA tutors explained in a *Guardian* newspaper article: 'When we were designing the course we canvassed coaches and asked them: if they could have been trained in anything to prepare for management, what would it have been? Often it was things like understanding balance sheets, but public speaking was a common response. They were used to talking to the media as players, but they were less comfortable standing up and giving presentations.'

The content of a team talk before, during or after the games, is one of the only areas of the modern game which has not been invaded by the media. The outside world will know little to nothing about the goings-on in the dressing room. The football world defends this with all their might. You will often hear the player or manager look steely-eyed at the camera while saying: 'That stays in the dressing room.' Sharing the words spoken, the details of heated exchanges or the tactical mastery is a cardinal sin. Like a magician revealing his tricks, it is something which should be unspoken, at least until the player or manager is long gone and looking for a hook to entice readers to their auto-biography.

Leaders in any walk of life will have team talks. We all have our half-time rants or mid-point adjustments to tactics. We all have a need to communicate alarm, surprise, urgency, despair, love, trust and all other forms of human emotion in order to inspire a desired response. For the supporter whose beloved team is losing, they may imagine a rabble-rousing speech akin to Mel Gibson in the movie Braveheart. While they pass the 15 minutes during the half-time break of a game, pouring the coffee from their flask or waiting impa-tiently in the hot dog queue they can imagine a blend of fury and tactical genius. As the old adage goes, football is most definitely a game of two halves and there is a common belief that the half-time talk defines the second of these halves.

In this chapter we will examine the power of team talks from those adept at delivering powerful speeches at key moments. We will also examine the theory and sometimes conflicting thoughts on the power of verbal and non-verbal communication.

Most importantly, we will draw on the lessons that leaders in the wider world can learn from this crucial aspect of the first 100 days and beyond. We will see that sometimes it is important to use words that are calm and consistent rather than eloquent and inspiring, in the face of adversity. Sometimes it is a case of just staying 'on message'. Sean Dyche gave us a unique insight as to what that might look like, in a toilet, mid-way during a Championship game!

The wisdom of a toilet wall in Wolverhampton

Prior to an away game against Wolverhampton Wanderers in the 2012-2013 season, Sean Dyche described feeling real stress for the first time as a manager. 'I don't get stressed really,' he explained, 'but that game against Wolves away was one that had been building up all week. It was the end of my first season and we'd been targeting the play-off positions but all of a sudden we were looking over our shoulders at the relegation zone after a couple of defeats. I remember going in at half-time and it really hit me. People might think that I gave a great speech or that I gave some great tactical advice that got us over the line in that game. I went into the toilet, just put my hands on the wall and said to myself: 'Breathe, breathe, breathe."

It was the penultimate game of the season and while his team were winning 1-0 at the interval, the fear of losing and slipping through the relegation trapdoor terrified him. Dyche continued: 'I pulled myself together and just said something to the players – I can't remember what. I just wanted them to get back out there and get us over the line. It was an experience that I got so much from. All the times I'd spent as a player at Bristol City, where they were booing me off and at Watford when people came to games with shirts saying 'Dyche out' helped give me the resilience to just get through it. When you're really up against it and everyone is looking at you, sometimes you just need to get through it. It wasn't clever words or anything like that. I just stuck to my usual plan and worked my way through the team, front to back. But the most important thing was just breathing and getting through it. The twist of the story is that we had a man sent off and had to play the last 20 minutes with 10 men! I remember our player walking off after the red and saying to myself: 'This is good for me, I'm calm and I'm thinking straight.' I just turned to my staff and we broke down what we were going to do.'

I asked what the difference would be if that situation was to arrive today, I wanted to know what had changed in his mindset. 'Experience,' Dyche replied. 'With experience you have been through it before. Simple as that. I'd be able to go back to the memory of that game and remember what I did. You learn from experience. I do a lot of self-talk.'

The notion of self-talk is a running dialogue that goes on inside the head of everyone during the course of the day. Leaders that are looking to constantly develop will process and learn from situations through self-talk. In conversation with Micky and Sean, it is clear that they both spend a lot of time with a running dialogue in their own head. As Dyche explained: 'This job can be a very isolating one. You spend a lot of time on your own and you've a lot of time to think.' With that in mind, it is clear that the time managers take to think is vital to manage effectively. Arguably, the time alone with your thoughts is a time when matches are won and lost. Sean Dyche is a manager who has clearly won many matches because he is acutely aware of the importance of managing his time, thoughts and wellbeing.

Managers are just people. They feel pressure, stress and emotion like anyone. When their backs are against the wall, the best managers will at times just cling on for dear life to get through that pressure moment and then learn from it.

On that day in Wolverhampton, despite having a man sent off with 20 minutes to go, Burnley won 2-1. 'It was like a pressure valve being opened and all that stress just drifted off. I made a mental note to remember that week, what got me through and what I'd need to do when moments like that came around again,' said Dyche. It is the resilience of the manager and his constant self-reflection that has helped develop Burnley. As leaders, sometimes in heated moments of pressure, you just need to keep calm and carry on. Delivering key messages can be crucial for more consistent impact over a long period of time. Sam Allardyce talked us though how he goes about getting the maximum output from his players by using specific language, tone and timing.

The power of words

Allardyce is meticulous in every aspect of his planning before a big game. His team of backroom staff analyse the performance, strength and statistics of his own players and of the opposition. In the modern game, there is very little that comes as a surprise in the top levels of football. Despite this, the variable of reality can derail the best-laid plans. Allardyce gives great thought to his pre-match and half-time team talks. He said: 'My words are short and sharp. A quick review of the strengths and weaknesses of the opposition. Before the big matches against the 'big boys' like away at Old Trafford or walking out at Anfield, you need to calm the players down. The teams that I think we should win against, I'm more aggressive to make sure there is no complacency.' Allardyce adjusts his messages accordingly. He notes the words and approach used and then reflects on how they affected each individual player, with hindsight and perhaps more importantly with data.

Allardyce's approach, in an educational parlance, could be described as 'data rich'. This extends to his use of words in the dressing room. 'If I'm ranting and raving all the time, it won't have the effect you want. You need to use it rarely. I've heard people say that you shouldn't shout at players because it might knock their confidence. My answer is simple – show me the data that tells me that. When you use that tactic of the hairdryer or whatever you want to call it, the data tells me that you get 15-20 minutes of improved performance. I'm not saying use it all the time but if you're going to tell me not to do it, I want to see the data that backs that up.'

The performance of a team is like a sunflower. The flower will grow in the right environment to a great height. However, various factors need to be in place to ensure it grows to its full potential. Firstly, the seed, and the ability of the seed to actually grow. In a football sense, can the players on the field actually deliver what is asked of them? Secondly, is the soil conducive to the growth of this flower? Thirdly, will the words used to direct and galvanise be the weather conditions required to stimulate that growth?

Crucially, the weather will change. The weather – the words of a team talk – can have a significant effect on the way that sunflower grows. However, the soil remains constant. The soil has evolved over a long period of time and while being affected by the weather, it will fundamentally remain. The first points here relate to recruitment and coaching which we looked at earlier in the book.

We will now address the words that provide the weather and examine how they can affect the team. We will then investigate how the relationships between the leader or manager and his team can be cultivated to ensure sustained growth in all weathers.

Sunflower Team Talks

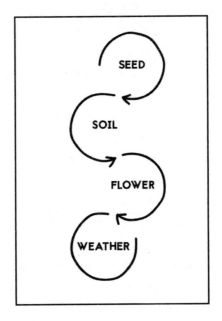

Words are the weather

Words provide the weather. Words access the minds and imagination of the players on the field. Words give immediate reaction and stimulate longer-term analysis and reflection. As the first 100 days moves quickly on, it is imperative that the weather created by our words creates a climate for a thriving working environment.

In 'Thinking Fast and Slow', Daniel Kahneman, a Nobel prize-winning behavioural psychologist, explains how words and the world around us affects two systems in our brain. System 1 is the intuitive, 'gut reaction' which could be described as the 'chimp' as you will remember from earlier chapters. System 2 is the analytical or computer-aspect of human thinking. System 1 forms powerful, 'instinctive' impressions and leads to emotive response to immediate stimulus, like a team talk. System 2 reflects and analyses.

Kahneman argues that we must be clear about the system we are looking to influence in order to communicate effectively. System 1 acts as a gate-keeper in order that System 2 can be unlocked to change behaviours over a sustained period of time. In the inspiring team talk, System 1 is engaged through a process Kahneman calls 'priming'. That is, key words are used to inspire action, energy and trust in the manager. Once this is established, System 2 can be entered in order to give the specific tactical and technical changes to the team's, office and department's operations.

In his seminal book, Kahneman references the now famous 'Florida effect' to epitomise the power priming words can have upon our self-conscience. The experiment, performed by psychologist John Bargh from New York University, asked students to assemble four-word sentences from a set of five words. The students were split into two groups. One group was given words relating to old age without specifically containing the word 'old' such as 'Florida', 'forgetful', 'bald', 'grey' or 'wrinkle'. The other group was given words which were neutral.

When they had completed the task, the participants were then asked to walk along a corridor which, unbeknown to them was part of the experiment. The participants were timed and those who had been working with the words relating to age walked slower than those who had not. When asked, the participants had not even realised that the words they were using were synonymous with age. However, they had been sub-consciously affected by the stimulus which primed their behaviour, as controlled by System 1. Kahneman explains that this phenomenon, known as the ideomotor effect, is the influencing of our actions by our ideas.

In a leader's first 100 days they must prime their teams, departments or organisations. Through words that energise rather than demoralise in an environment which fosters safety and aspiration in equal measure.

Learning to S.U.M.O. (Shut Up, Move On)

In the arena of self-leadership, resilience and dealing with change, *Sunday Times* best-selling author Paul McGee is a leading thinker and speaker across both the UK and abroad.

Paul's most successful book, 'S.U.M.O (Shut Up, Move On): The Straight-Talking Guide to Succeeding in Life', has helped hundreds of thousands of people around the world that have either read the text or heard Paul speak. His work has also inspired the team talks of leading sports coaches. This book is one of 11 written by Paul with a further two to follow in the next year. His core message is that it is possible to take ownership of the situations around us that can influence our sense of wellbeing. For the football manager, business leader or the like, Paul offers a blueprint for us to accept, then 'Shut Up' and 'Move On'. The blueprint is illustrated in his now enigmatic postcard.

The S.U.M.O. Model
Seven questions to help you Shut Up and Move On

1. Where is this issue on a scale of 1-10?
2. How important will this be in six months' time?
3. Is my response appropriate and effective?
4. How can I influence or improve the situation?
5. What can I learn from this?
6. What will I do differently next time?
7. What can I find that's positive in this situation?

The key to Paul's model is to analyse and reflect on situations. Maintaining perspective is crucial. He explains that in answering question 1, you should consider 10 on the scale as being death! Everything else decreases in actual severity. The subsequent questions encourage reflection, thinking, solution-focused discussions, a learning process and ultimately positive change. This is a framework to channel and process thoughts and can be used by leaders in challenging situations. As Paul repeatedly says to his audiences: 'Words change worlds'. So it is important that we choose our thoughts and words wisely, especially in the first 100 days.

Setting the temperature inside the Etihad

Paul and I met to discuss the strategies that managers and others can use to cope with the stresses and strains of leadership and life. He told me: 'I believe that well-being leads to well-doing. Well-being within leaders and those we work with is not just a nice thing to have. It's not just something that is necessary during a pandemic for example, it is central to everything that we do on a daily basis.'

One of Paul's great strengths is his ability to offer tools to the listener or reader that can be used to have a positive impact on our lives and the lives of others around us. As we sipped coffee during our online meeting, he shared an analogy with me that made so much sense and captured the very essence of leading an organisation in an emotionally healthy way. Paul explained: 'You are the thermostat and the thermometer. Your mood and morale impacts everyone else. Like a thermostat, you set the mood and check it. Along with that, you also need to take the temperature and adjust the thermostat frequently.'

Paul extended the analogy. 'You've got to service the thermostat though. That requires building in rest and time to re-energize. Stress makes you stupid and you make snap decisions that can negatively influence the temperature.'

Paul's work has had a significant impact upon the football world. He has had a 10-year relationship with Manchester City and their players. For five years, he was on a monthly retainer at the club. He worked with the playing and coaching staff. His impact was such that his S.U.M.O. postcard was displayed with club colours on the training ground wall. He spent a significant amount of time working with Patrick Vieira, Shay Given and the now current Burnley captain Ben Mee as well as other big-name players at the club. His work supported the team as they headed towards their first Premier League title in 2012.

The 'Comms Wrapper'

Team talks and mantras such as S.U.M.O. can establish the credibility of a leader. In business and education, as in football, the key messages must reach the people within the organisation and those stakeholders watching on externally. This balance was central to Mark Palios' experience of a successful first 100 days. 'You've got your internal and your external priorities. You've got to manage your external priorities closely, especially with an organisation that works with the public. However, if you don't keep a close eye on your internal priorities then you'll quickly lose credibility within. Both are really important.'

What Palios described as a 'Comms Wrapper' was effectively the team talks of big business. These team talks recognised the need to share with the public, shareholders or local community the external priorities which are important to those involved in or with the organisation. The internal priorities are the agenda which allows for these external priorities to be realized. For example, to improve the results of a team, the manager may be talking about styles of play and getting back to the training ground. However, the internal priorities may well be a turnover of the players on the pitch.

It comes back to the importance of credibility as discussed earlier. For Palios, the first 100 days revolved around developing, building and then maintaining this. He would go on to explain how he kept an eye on the internal and external temperature in order to maintain a balance. A loss of confidence in his organisation from onlookers or insiders could have a detrimental impact upon the first 100 days.

Day 54 – nervous before a big test

At St Bede's I thought I had created an atmosphere of confidence, security and ambition. I hoped it was similar to that created by Ole Gunnar Solskjær after hearing about the impact he has had at Manchester United.

Day to day, I think I could say that was true. The feedback from staff was that they felt secure in giving their opinions and that their opinions would be heard. I would often have honest and open conversations with staff who had concerns or issues they wished to raise. As well as our teaching team, I would also gauge the support team's views from our Business and HR Manager, Annette Southworth.

However, on Day 54, I stood in our dining hall discussing

school with an experienced member of our teaching staff. She asked me a pertinent question. 'Why haven't you talked to us about Ofsted? We know they're coming and to be honest we all feel a bit nervous about it. It feels like we're not going to be prepared for when they finally arrive.'

It was a sentiment I had not picked up on. Ofsted is the body which acts on behalf of the Department for Education to inspect schools. The judgement of Ofsted can have a big impact on a school's popularity with parents and the community, as well as affecting the careers of headteachers and other teaching staff – and even impacting local house prices. These judgements are constructed during a one or two-day inspection of a school which can be a very intense experience.

Our staff did not feel prepared for this.

I quickly organised a meeting the following week to talk through the plans we had developed as a leadership team. We were, in fact, very ready and I had deliberately not talked about an inspection because everything we were doing was actually preparing us; the standards we had set were aligned with an inspection focus.

Day 56 – inspired by Micky and Sam

My message about Ofsted, during a 15-minute Friday morning briefing, was short and simple. I shared our Ofsted preparation plan with our teaching staff. It was meticulous. It covered every action we would take minute by minute from when we got the Ofsted call. We had planned who would do what and when.

At the end I had one slide with three points that I would share with them so that they could do their part in supporting the school during the inspection. Later in the year, I would give that same presentation the night before we had our inspection. We followed our plan to the minute. The result was a calm process that was highly successful. So many staff spoke to me about how calm and fluent the whole experience was. It was a real team effort on the day but it was the plan that made our approach and delivery so effective. This plan was kicked off with a calm team talk that took the heat out of the situation – inspired by the words of Sam Allardyce describing an away trip to Old Trafford and Micky describing a lower league rivalry, with no less passion and desire to succeed.

Parents in the workplace and 'losing the dressing room'

The same message can be delivered in the same way, with the same words, in the same tone, in the same room with entirely different outcomes. The leader must create a sense of safety and belonging amongst the team. This should not be confused with a soft environment that does not demand high standards. Rather, it is an environment which is fertile for brutal honesty underpinned by authentic trust.

Micky exemplified what this looked like at Tranmere in the 2018-2019 season following a crushing 6-0 away defeat to Shrewsbury Town. In a post-match interview, he said: 'I love all my players and I want them to do really, really well. That's the disappointing thing.' This was not a one-off and this message of love is something that often pervades

Micky's media interviews. It is perhaps a side of the modern manager which is not appreciated. In Simon Sinek's book, 'Leaders Eat Last', he alludes to highly effective leaders as being like parents in the workplace. That is, they want the best for their colleagues and show belief in the potential of those in the work family. This comes from a place of love and respect, considering people as individuals. It is something that comes across clearly when top managers such as Jürgen Klopp and Pep Guardiola talk to the media about their players.

Such an environment changes the context of the rabble-rousing speeches or 'rollockings' which may also be required to generate an intense response. Mark Cooper, manager of Forest Green, described one such speech delivered by Micky as Tranmere returned to the away changing room after a poor first-half display. Cooper said: 'You know what's coming, they're going to get an almighty rollocking at half-time, which they did. I could hear it and you know they're going to come at you.' Crucially, the sense of anger comes from a place that the players feel a belonging and the sort of disappointment a parent can feel towards their child who has made a poor decision.

The sense of care and love from the members of any team effectively primes them to understand messages from the leader as being ones of support and care rather than of threat and menace. The latter can lead to individual feelings of low self-worth and a lack of confidence. As a group, the effect of a lack of belonging can be mistrust, a sense of betrayal and ultimately lead to the manager 'losing the dressing room'.

The allegation that a manager has lost the dressing room is often referred to by pundits and the circling media who await the next managerial casualty. Football managers and all leaders must create an environment of safety and belonging in order to give themselves the best chance of falling foul of this accusation.

Losing the 'top' table at Carrington

Ole Gunnar Solskjær was acutely aware of the need to address the environment at Carrington in order to re-assert the 'United Way' that he felt had been lost in recent years. Despite being a firm favourite amongst the fans and loved by the club's hierarchy, Ole was only really seen as a short-term fix until the 'right' man became available. 'We just said enjoy every day and see what happens,' said Ole, with Mick Phelan adding: 'But from pretty early on we actually thought we could make things better here and we wanted it for longer.' Still, his managerial credentials paled in comparison to the previous three incumbents: David Moyes, Louis Van Gaal and José Mourinho. The latter two of the three had won everything there was to win in the game with the biggest clubs in the world. Solskjær had endured a disappointing tenure as manager of Cardiff City but found success in the Norwegian League with Molde. Ole won the Tippeligaen (the Norwegian top tier) in his first two seasons there and returned for a moderately successful spell after his stint at Cardiff. But this did not make him an obvious choice as a long-term appointment for one of the biggest football clubs in the world.

After eight wins in a row on the field, though, he became the front runner for the job. Media commentators were already asking: 'Who would actually want to follow someone who's had such an incredible start?'

The wins on the field were only part of the turnaround that Ole was inspiring at the club. As we sat in the coaches' office at Carrington, I asked him about the differences between the culture in his time as a player and what he returned to as manager in December 2018. We sat around a Subbuteo table with two teams on the felt pitch (a red one and a sky blue one, of course!). Ole smiled and said: 'There were so many differences. I've got a list!' Then he stood up and beckoned Micky and I towards the door. As he opened it, the corridor with a glass wall faced onto the team canteen. 'See that table there? When I first arrived it was empty and everyone was eating and chatting on all the other tables.' The tables were set out in rows to the right of the breakfast bars and coffee machines. The 'top' table was the one that Ole pointed to. 'I sat with all the lads and asked why no-one sat at that table. They said: 'That's the management team's table'. I thought to myself – 'that's just not Manchester United." Quickly, just by sitting with the players and staff, Ole had brought the club back to the 'industrial' tradition that everyone was in it together. 'It wasn't difficult for me really. We were just being ourselves,' he added.

Often players are given managerial roles on the basis of their successful playing careers or the experience of playing under respected managers and coaches. In Ole's situation, it was his Norwegian managerial success and personality alongside these past triumphs on the pitch which landed him the role at United. In the world of business, you can be promoted due to success on the shop floor, only to find that the set of skills for the job you are promoted to bear no relation to your previous position. I have found this in the world of education. Success in the classroom does not prepare a teacher for the challenges of headship that include financial awareness, employment law, HR structures, public speaking, recruitment and a myriad of other challenges. What gets you to a leadership role will not necessarily be what keeps you there. For Ole, it was his awareness of culture, environment and emotional intelligence which proved invaluable assets.

Day 58 – over to you

Schools can often run at 100 mph. On Day 58, we were due to have a three-hour training inset at the end of the day. The staff were concerned about other deadlines so our Deputy Headteacher, Dan Morgan, and our Assistant Headteacher Deb Harris suggested we cancel the planned training session and instead give the time to our teaching staff to plan their own training on the areas they felt were really pressing. I thought back to a conversation with Micky about listening to key players on the pitch and I took Dan and Deb's advice.

The sense of relief and release from the staff was tangible as we walked around the building. It was a decision that showed an emotional intelligence and reflected a trust in the independent will of our staff to be part of a self-improving school system.

Carlo's way – creating team 'safety'

In organisations, with football teams being no exception, there are recurring signs of safety which can be identified. In his book 'Culture Code', Daniel Coyle researched a wide range of organisations in an effort to identify and highlight signs of institutional safety. He found that common signs were close physical proximity, plenty of eye contact, energetic exchanges, mixing of groups, lots of questions with few interruptions to the answers, active listening, laughter and lots of small courtesies.

Coyle describes how studies have shown that a significant influencing factor in the creativity of office teams was the proximity of employees' desks to each other. It may sound obvious but being together, talking, listening, respecting and effectively understanding each other is imperative to create a sense of safety. Within the 'soil of safety' truly great things can happen as members of the team or group become cohesive and develop a sense of trust.

'When you encounter a group with good chemistry, you know it instantly,' said Coyle.

He references the great US basketball coach Gregg Popovich who delivered magical, impactful feedback to his team in a variety of ways. Occasionally this would be in a loud and aggressive form in order to instigate a rapid response mid-game. Popovich knew, though, that this feedback was all the more powerful due to the intense sense of belonging the players felt towards him. As Coyle explains, the feedback was based on the premise that 'you are part of this group, this group is special, we have the highest standards and I believe you can reach these standards.' If the mid-game messages were delivered in the form of yelling, they actually filled the players with greater belief due to the authentic belief that the coach had in the ability of his players.

In his book 'Quiet Leadership', Carlo Ancelotti, with the help of Chris Brady and Mike Forde, outlines his process for developing a sense of safety and belonging. Ancelotti is regarded as one of the best and most successful managers of all time. His starting point is to speak to the players, workers and colleagues as people first and foremost. Rather than addressing your finance officer as the person controlling the money, speak to them as the single mother or bike-riding enthusiast first before addressing their performance in the role they are in. Such an approach fosters a relationship over time which can lead to a sense of safety and belonging that gives the best chance of high performance.

Ancelotti stresses that we do not control those we work with, regardless of our position of authority. Rather we provide the right information for them to achieve their full potential. Referring back to earlier chapters, the right people must be on the bus to begin with. As Ancelotti stresses: 'The 'how do we drive the bus?' comes after 'who made the driver of the bus?'' He is not alone in this approach.

Stephen Covey's 'Seven Habits of Highly Effective People' identifies habit five as being: 'Seek first to understand, then to be understood.' Covey explains that the trap that many leaders fall into is that: 'Most people do not listen with the intent to understand; they listen with the intent to reply.'

Throughout his book, Ancelotti explains how he is open, listens and shows that he cares about the players and staff and their families as people. As a leader, he is highly effective at this, which is confirmed by several of the game's greatest players to have played under him. Cristiano Ronaldo explains how, '...he's very humble, which is not so normal in the football business. He treats everybody as an equal. He never dismisses someone just because they are not at his level; he will always listen.' The crucial aspect of developing a sense of safety and belonging in the first 100 days and beyond is to listen, to understand, to show humility, to show a love before the leader makes the discerning effort to become understood. Whether it is Cristiano Ronaldo, Zlatan Ibrahimovic, John Terry or Seamus Coleman, the players talk with a sense of love and family. It is this sense of belonging and safety that creates the environment conducive to the growth of a team, the rising of the sunflower through the soil of safety and the words that create the weather.

World Cup winner Sir Clive is still curious

I asked Paul McGee, the author of S.U.M.O. who we met in an earlier chapter, what messages he gives to clubs and organisations in order to support the sort of culture that can win titles or achieve success in all manner of fields. He explained: 'I target the characters Damian Hughes describes as 'cultural architects'. These are the people that influence the others in the group. In meetings, I suggest that leaders use an agenda that channels positive thinking about the successes and challenges that face the group.'

Paul explained the three things he believes prompt positive thought: 'Firstly, I ask what is working well. Then we discuss what individuals are working on and how they're looking to improve themselves and the team. Finally, I ask what we can do, as an organisation or as leaders, to help this improvement.' In teams where they feel that such coaching or development is not required, Paul uses sporting analogies such as tennis. 'I point to the world's best tennis players such as Rafa Nadal, Roger Federer, Novak Djokovic or Andy Murray. They have a coach, they have a support team, they analyse every part of their game and they adapt it to be the best it can possibly be.'

Like many of the managers we spoke to, he stressed the need to remain humble and curious as a leader. Paul gave another example. 'When Sir Clive Woodward went to Southampton, he contacted me and asked me to come and help him gain a fresh perspective on his approach. A World Cup-winning coach, he wanted me to give him an alternative voice. He was modelling the desire for constant improvement as a leader that he hoped to share across the club.' As leaders, this desire for constant improvement is essential in creating a Kaizen culture which is filled with optimism, positivity and hope from Day 1 to 100 and beyond.

The strength of vulnerability

The approach described by Paul, the openness to support and different perspectives is crucial to 360 degree thinking and leading. However, this openness can be seen as a weakness or a vulnerability by some individuals.

In many quarters, it is expected that the football manager has the answers to the tactical dilemmas, the secrets to acute emotional intelligence and a foresight to plan financially in order that he will lead the club to immediate victories and longer-term glories. This can be the view of anyone within an organisation when a new leader begins and can create a distance between the leader and their team. Each is evaluating the other and reaching opinions that are driven by the System 1 described by Kahneman. Too often, leaders fall foul of maintaining this distance and leading from afar in an effort to keep themselves on the pedestal that their new position has initially bestowed.

Both Daniel Coyle in 'Culture Code' and Berné Brown in 'Dare to Lead' point to overwhelming evidence that suggests that the first step to creating a group sense of belonging is vulnerability. This may at first appear counter intuitive, as it suggests that leaders should establish strength through showing their weakness.

After a disappointing 1-1 draw at home to non-league Oxford City, Micky sat his players in a circle to discuss the significantly under-par performance. This could have been the opportunity to call out all of the players' mistakes and poor performance. However, Micky opened up a conversation which showed his vulnerability.

He explained: 'We sat down and talked through the running stats. They had not covered as much ground as usual. I said to them: 'If you don't run we're finished. You are finished and I am finished.' They had to know that that type of performance was going to end in us all losing our jobs. I'd lose mine and they'd all see their careers go downhill. So without putting the blame on anyone, we were all part of sorting this out.'

Coyle describes this as the Vulnerability Loop. The loop cultivates a common trust through the sharing of vulnerabilities. This, Coyle argues, is the building a sense of belonging and underpinning effective co-operation between the group.

The Vulnerability Loop

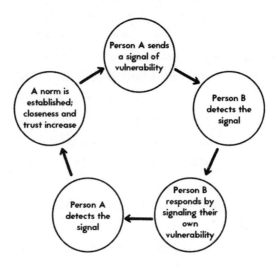

Quickly sharing vulnerability appropriately allows the leader to develop trust quickly in the first 100 days. It avoids a sense that the leader is an island who will seek to find the solutions themselves and subsequently take the glory for themselves as well. The leader must be vulnerable first and often within a context of high standards and a relentless drive to improve. Top-level managers will skilfully choose their moments to take the blame for picking the wrong tactics in order to defuse criticism which may be directed towards the team and also show the team that there is a collective responsibility and culture that is one of trust and not blame. Some ideas for appropriate expressions are detailed below to help you consider how you might signal vulnerability when undertaking your first 100 days.

Vulnerability Signals

Signal: This is only my idea, what do you think?
Common response or impact: Either an alternate point of view or engagement in the proposed idea.

Signal: How have you seen this work effectively before?
Common response or impact: Group discussion and shared ownership of a solution.

Leader's Signal: Tell me what you think could go wrong with this strategy?
Common response or impact: Inviting critique and offering an opportunity for concerns to be shared.

Leader's Signal: You probably have more experience in this area, tell me you've seen this work before ...
Common response or impact: Offering power to the team member to lead the strategy and showing belief in the ability.

Football managers and leaders in general must do their

best to find the vulnerabilities which may hinder their efforts to galvanise and lead those around them. In order to seek out vulnerabilities, I have often used analytical tools which ask colleagues from across the school or organisation to offer their thoughts on the leader's communication, ideology and many other aspects of their approach. The feedback can stimulate reflection and revised actions.

The unknown vulnerabilities are commonly referred to as 'blind spots'. That is, those vulnerabilities not seen by the leader but seen in full vision by those around them. In the world of football, feedback is not something which has to be sought on a match day. There are thousands in attendance and subsequently contributing to the various online and radio forums, only too happy to explain the errors of the manager's ways. However misguided and ill-informed some opinions may be, they are opinions nevertheless.

Micky pays close attention to the online voices. He explains: 'I do have social media accounts. Twitter and the like are brilliant to gain information about new approaches to coaching, rehabilitation or world class setpieces. I don't have my name on my account but I also use it to have a wee look at what the fans are saying. I see what their perceptions are of what's going on at the club and on the pitch. It helps me to get my messages right when I'm facing the press.'

Using this insight, Micky can quash an unfounded belief that the club has a league-topping budget or that there are plans to settle for mid-table mediocrity. He also sees what the opinion of fans is toward certain players and will point out the unseen efforts that may otherwise go unnoticed.

At St Bede's, the perception of the parents and some onlookers was that the school was only focused on exam results. This was far from the truth and the efforts of the committed teachers and support staff deserved much more recognition. With the help of willing colleagues, I set up a blog which details the success stories of students and teams. It also showcases a broad curriculum which was far from being solely exam-focused. The blog and subsequent Twitter and Instagram pages allow departments to show off their commitment to a school which offers a holistic education for the students. Since this has come into force, there has no longer been criticism from parents along the lines of 'all you care about is getting kids to do exams'. Whether it is addressing parents, shareholders or football supporters, it is essential to address these perceptions to create an external sense of confidence and trust in the leader. This will not guarantee success but it will offer the best chance of creating an environment geared to achieving that.

Servant leaders and self-motivated teams

When Micky and I discussed leadership during the first 100 days and beyond we regularly came back to the notion of service.

'I remind myself that I'm here to improve the players and at Dundee United, like Tranmere, we've got an incredible group desperate to improve every day. I'm here for the club and the supporters. We're all here for that. That helps me to be objective and consistent in the big conversations. When you're dropping a player, telling them they need to improve or even preparing them for retirement, I start by reminding myself of my role and why I'm here.'

Micky can give several examples of this approach. He recounts a common conversation with a player out of the squad.

'I had a player come in my office to ask me why he was not playing. I kept to these principles. I explained 'I'm here for the club and the fans but I'm also here for the player'. I'm honest and I care about them, I give a damn if they get better or not. If you're not genuine, if you're not serving the club and everyone associated with it then you'll soon get found out. It's the same when we comb over video analysis of the last match. I tell the players I care about them, their careers and their families, that's why I'm so honest with them. They need to know and we all need to tell each other, in the right way, what the truth is.'

This approach can be seen in some of the world's great leaders through time; Ghandi, Mandela or Obama. They all conveyed a sense of servant leadership, that their purpose was to serve those they led rather than for their followers to serve them. That is not to say that these leaders lacked strength, charisma, confidence and drive. Rather, great football managers and leaders in general give their followers a sense that they are connected, important and part of a special movement.

Servant leaders are often honest to a fault and maintain a clear vision in all they do. Indeed, servant leadership encourages self-organising teams that can operate without the presence of the leader at all times. The members of the team become leaders in their own right, operating with autonomy and ownership. Ask Micky what his leadership goal is and he will tell you succinctly: 'To make myself redundant.' Though this may sound counter-intuitive, what Micky desires is a team that can self-organise, self-regulate and self-motivate.

It is perhaps one area in which we disagree. I do believe a leader may become operationally redundant on a short-term basis, however, a figurehead leader is always required for the long-term, the strategic and the personification of a vision. Micky concurred: 'I can become operationally redundant day to day. It's a bit like flying a plane. I am needed for the take-off and the landing but if you've got the principles nailed down, you can release your staff and players to run on autopilot when you're not there. That's what I mean, really, about becoming 'redundant'. The last thing I mean is that I become complacent, it's not that at all.'

Day 62 – small things matter

As we headed towards Christmas, a break for me and the busiest period of the season for Micky, we again dined with Head of Sports Science Andy Hodgen. Andy shared his leadership style with Micky and I. 'I'm just the same as you guys in my role. I head up the fitness but I'm there to help the players. It's easy to do that when you're winning but try telling them which shake to drink after you've lost the game. You need to remind them why you're there.' Andy was exactly right and both Micky and I agreed that as a manager and headteacher, we too were servant leaders.

The next day I spent 10 minutes after arriving at school listing the ways I was serving my team and the school more broadly. There were big things and small things. Of course, the time given to the job, strategic planning and delivery were an expected 'service'. However, I recalled speaking with middle leaders and students who had noted the smaller things, such as making people a cup of tea before meetings, covering duties or lessons to support a colleague and helping our site staff put the chairs away after a late evening event. All of these things represent a servant leadership.

Micky and I had long talked about this idea of service. 'I'd never realised this was a thing people had coined. It's just being a good person and doing what you're there to do,' he explained over an Indian meal. Before Christmas, I was determined to make sure that I maintained the same level of service leadership to continue progressing my role.

While Micky is a charismatic leader with authority and authenticity, he has created a team around him that embodies the skills and characteristics encouraged by the principles of servant leadership. As per this approach he is an enabler whose leadership includes a paternal streak which he would argue is more 'big brother' than 'fatherly'. Without doubt, his focus is on improving and celebrating others like any caring elder sibling or father figure would.

Dependent on results, people will perceive servant leadership as the character of a weak or courageous leader. However, servant leadership is arguably the most effective underpinning approach for sustained long-term development during and beyond the first 100 days.

'Let me enjoy my wine tonight' – celebrate success

In the process of Micky and I writing this book, we spoke a lot about giving yourself the best chance of success. It is a topic that all leaders will no doubt consider. One area that I had not really considered importantly, at least consciously so, was what happens when you win. Micky challenged me to consider what I do, as head teacher, when we as a school achieve something good.

Initially, I was defensive in my response and pointed to references to our successes in briefings. I talked about presentations that highlighted our relative performance. I did not, however, *celebrate* the victories. I did not give our team time to enjoy the success they had worked so hard for. It had to change. Perhaps this was the biggest failing of my first 100 days.

Upon reflection, I believe this was down to a fear of complacency amongst the team who may believe that the job was done and they could step off the gas. But this was not the sort of 'brave leadership' talked of in Berné Brown's 'Dare to Lead'. Rather, this reflected my own feelings of anxiety and vulnerability that can ultimately lead to decline. Upon speaking with our Head of English, I found that by not celebrating success, some colleagues felt an anti-climax and a lack of appreciation. No words can then undo that feeling.

Our school will now celebrate our successes and ensure that we enjoy them as a group. Following a victory, when a journalist will automatically ask about preparations for the next challenge, Micky and other managers might say:

'Let me enjoy my glass of wine tonight, I'll think about that tomorrow.' As a leader it is imperative to enjoy the highs because failure to do so is not a healthy way for you to feel and for your team, office or group to be treated.

Day 65 – saying thanks

On this day, I planned a series of quick chats with staff to share my gratitude for their work and achievements. I also made a point of kicking every week off by thanking the staff for their work the week before and talking about individuals that had supported colleagues or led specific events. I focused on really celebrating the positives as well as talking about what we can do to improve.

Later on in the year, Micky's words rang in my ears after our successful Ofsted inspection. Rather than a simple 'well done', we arranged a staff buffet and celebration. This idea of really celebrating the positive can lift an organisation, it is a lesson I took from football and one which will stay with me long beyond the first 100 days.

Life is tough, so is work, so if you're the leader you have to look to bring a sense of joy when the going is good. Whether in work or at home, it is important to stop in that moment and just take a breath to enjoy a sense of collective and individual achievement.

There's more to life . . .

As we headed toward Christmas, the first 100 days of my tenure was proving to be successful. I had a clarity in my thinking about what we would be achieving.

While this was happening, though, I had been consumed with the job. This consumption had led to me neglecting my role as a husband and father. I had been home late and, while I was there on occasion in body, I was rarely fully present in mind. It was really taking a toll on my family.

This is a topic that so many leadership books or gurus neglect: what about the people who are suffering at home because of a leader's total investment in work? I had to do something about this. If I did not, I knew the long-term effects of this would be dire on my wife and family. Ultimately, the cost of neglecting your own wellbeing and that of your nearest and dearest, can have a very negative effect on a leader's ability to be effective.

More importantly, the cost of professional success can be a lack of personal fulfilment and poor mental and emotional health. As I moved forward in my first 100 days, I realised I needed to achieve more of a personal work/life balance.

Reflections

1. When do you deliver team talks?

2. What words will you use to reinforce your key vision and action messages?

3. How will you create an environment of safety?

4. How will that environment foster a sense of belonging?

5. How will you serve your team?

6. How can you communicate this service?

7. What are the fears of your team and how can you create a healthy sense of safety? That is, not a sense of complacency but a sense that you believe in them to excel.

8. *How successfully do you believe you can make yourself redundant as an operational manager?*

9. *Where will you show vulnerability and service in your leadership?*

10. *What is success for your team and how do you celebrate this?*

Chapter Nine

DAYS 66-79

 Managing the manager

Pep talk – be true to yourself

As a leader in any capacity it is clear to those in our team or watching from the sidelines whether an approach is authentic or not. Pep Guardiola will repeatedly tell coaches or leaders that attend a seminar with him: 'Don't copy and paste me.' In other words, you must be yourself. While as a leader or an aspiring leader in any field there will be influential people in our lives, it is essential to stay true to the values that suit our character and personality.

In my field of teaching, we deal with the most honest and harshest of critics when it comes to authenticity, children. Children can disregard the teacher who has their best interests at heart which can often result in poor behaviour in the classroom. The same is true within a football club, office or boardroom. For a leader to be themselves requires an awareness of the characteristics that have led them to this point. To be oneself is not enough, a leader must then see how the strengths that they possess will support their ability to follow the steps toward a successful first 100 days.

Furthermore, successful leaders must understand their own vulnerabilities. A great example of this is given to us by the many steely managers of Glasgow who have displayed an inner strength and resilience. This toughness of character is born out of a childhood laden with adversity and challenge. The story of these men teaches us much about the value of struggle in the development of leaders.

Learning from the giants of Glasgow

The streets of some Glaswegian council estates can be laden with the obstacles of economic hardship, social deprivation, organised crime and sectarian violence. Films and television dramas will often portray a cold, grey, gritty realism to the narratives that are lived out by the proud people of this multi-layered city. Yet, Glasgow is also a city of culture, community and family. The dichotomy of a Glaswegian childhood is perhaps best described by arguably her most famous son, Billy Connolly, who sang:

'…Oh but Glasgow gave me more
Than it ever took away
And prepared me for life on the road'

The mixture of love and hate that defines the city of Glasgow, perhaps more than any other in the UK, has created football managers that have indeed been prepared for 'a life on the road'. The city has produced some of the finest managers of all time. These leaders include Jock Stein, Sir Matt Busby, Sir Alex Ferguson, George Graham and Sir

Kenny Dalglish. Other highly successful managers including Walter Smith, David Moyes, Alex McLeish and Micky himself credit much of their success to the city that formed their sense of resilience, ambition, grit and determination. In this chapter we will examine the strength that adversity can develop in leaders of any field. We will address the blind spots that any upbringing can create and we will see how great leaders in football utilise their life lessons to form an authenticity to their leadership style.

What trauma teaches

'Growing up in Glasgow taught me a lot. We left the house in the morning and came back when it was dark. We had no supervision, we had no-one telling us what to do or protect us if we got into any type of bother. It was a life that taught me to be very vigilant. It taught me to read people and situations. It taught me to be confident and appear strong, regardless of the situation. It taught me to know where the nearest exit was in any pub I went in to and what the chances of me needing to take it in a hurry!' explains Micky.

The Dundee United manager grew up on a council estate and learnt quickly to be street wise and alert to the environment around him. Micky credits his ability as a manager to read people and situations directly to his early childhood experiences. 'My wife and I could go into a bar or a nightclub and she'd be up and dancing away. I'd be looking around thinking 'this doesn't feel right'. I'd tell her we're getting out of here and she'd ask 'why?'. The next day we'd hear how it all kicked off in there and I couldn't tell you how I knew it would, I just knew it would.' The years of youth that were riddled with hard lessons for mistaken loyalty or trust, have taught and equipped Micky to be able to react in the most effective manner in every situation. 'I'd be walking a mile and a half to school on my own from the age of four. It teaches you to be aware of your surroundings and to see any dangers that might be ahead.' Growing up in Glasgow also allowed Micky to become a social chameleon who could change his tone, speech, body language and words to suit the situation. He recognises this strength and uses it with confidence to deal with players, agents, supporters, owners and the media.

Former Scotland manager Alex McLeish also believes that life in Glasgow can equip managers to be strong and resilient. Talking to the BBC, McLeish explained: 'It's in the DNA ... there was a definite determination to succeed. My dad was a sore loser and that probably rubbed off on me as well.' David Moyes elaborated further in the same article. 'You had to look after yourself in Glasgow ... that didn't mean you had to be the best fighter, it just meant you had to look after yourself, whether that meant you had the sharpest tongue, or you were a fast runner and could run away from people, or you could handle yourself.' Moyes went on to explain: 'The environment in Glasgow made me want to get involved in football. At that time there was nothing else. It was football or nothing. You played in the park on a Sunday and with your pals at night in the street. I didn't really know anything else.'

Whether it is Glasgow, London, Wigan or Belfast, we all

gain qualities from our childhood. We gain characteristics that have given us the capability to succeed in whatever sphere we operate within.

Carlo Ancelotti had a very different upbringing to that of managers growing up on a council estate. Ancelotti grew up in a rural Italian cheese-farming town named Reggiolo. The town, in the heartlands of northern Italy, is now famous for both its Parmesan cheese and their world famous manager. Ancelotti learned from his father Giuseppe that great things could be achieved with a cheerful, amiable and grounded personality. It was this ability to treat people with respect and dignity that allowed Ancelotti to form such special bonds with players who in return would play with passion and commitment. While Ancelotti used his personality to create and develop caring relationships with his players, he gained their trust and respect through an expertise born from the example set by his hard-working father and mother. By leading with an authenticity of personality and the authority of knowledge, Ancelotti grounded his leadership success in his true self.

In order to 'know thyself' leaders must know what their character strengths are and utilise these attributes in order to capture this authentic leadership. They must ensure that these characteristics are used especially as the course is set for the first 100 days.

When this happens, alongside the steps described earlier in this book, leaders can lead as themselves within a considered approach that is fit for the situation they find themselves within.

Family first

During our time with Ole Gunnar Solskjær and Mick Phelan, we did not specifically talk about the idea of 'looking after yourself' or 'managing number one'. However, halfway through our afternoon together, Ole's phone rang. As he walked away putting the phone to his ear, he told us: 'It's the Mrs. Sorry chaps, she's the most important one!' As it was a non-training day, he wore jeans with a loose fitting jumper. Over his shoulder was a satchel containing his work for the day. He smiled, was relaxed and looked like he was in his element. Later that evening, Ole would stay to watch his son play for United's Under-12s team.

As in his press conferences and when he is seen pitchside during games, Ole was calm and a realist during our meeting. 'It is probably because of my Norwegian upbringing,' he explained. 'I just work hard and do my best every day. I want to enjoy myself and have fun. That's what Mick and I said when we arrived.' Of course, the enjoyment comes with a great work ethic and a quiet ruthlessness in the quest for winning matches. Such qualities only add to the manager's credibility. He models a healthy balance between drive, ambition and taking care of those around him. It was clear as we walked through the corridors of Carrington, he was not interested in labouring in the past; he looked forward to the future while being true to the club's heritage and traditions.

Similarly, Mick Phelan also modelled this humble, calm approach. Mick sat with jeans on and white casual shirt untucked. Just like Ole, he was relaxed and completely at ease in his surroundings. 'I still live where I've always lived. When I came here I thought that it would be fun, I had something to give and if it didn't work out I'd go back to Australia to work on what I was doing out there,' he told us. 'I like living where I live because you can get away from things. You get a nice pint in the pubs,' he smiled. He was at peace with his achievements and ability while also having that quiet, innate, fiery ambition to begin a new chapter for the club they both loved deeply.

Sitting with the managerial duo, I saw how relaxed they were in their own ability and positions. They were the leaders of, arguably, the biggest football club on the planet. Yet, you could be forgiven for thinking they were two guys off the street just talking about their hobby. That is not to undersell their tactical knowledge and wealth of experience, which they also exuded, it is simply to reflect their conscious competence and genuine happiness in the professional lives they were living.

From our meeting with Mick and Ole, I adopted their calm, measured and considered approach to leadership. They knew the zone of operation, they authentically shared a vision for the club and they were more concerned with the organisation/team than they were about their own professional interests. They believed in this club and this club believed in them. However, they did not allow their professional hunger to overwhelm their personal lives. This again epitomised why they were the right people to lead a football club that was based on family, loyalty, tradition and an industrial work ethic.

Sleepless nights and the mental health 'five a day'

Both Sam Allardyce and Joe Royle talked to Micky about the pressures of the first 100 days. Allardyce was adamant that the first 100 days is without doubt the hardest period of a manager's tenure due to the rate of change and the development of relationships required to achieve the desired change. Royle spoke with Micky about the amount of family time lost and the nights of broken sleep due to a poor result. Both Joe and Sam described how they analysed every factor in the game and scrutinised every decision after a defeat. Micky and I sat and spoke about the pressures that all leaders feel when the lights go out and they are left only with the darkness and thoughts of what might have been had different decisions have been made. Whether you're a head-teacher, a football manager or a CEO, expect these sleepless nights, particularly in those first 100 days. Leaders must accept but rationalise these thoughts as part of a lifestyle and thought process conducive to good mental health.

Experts now point to a 'five a day' requirement for strong mental health. Like anyone in life, leaders are not immune to the pressures and strains of life which can result in anxiety, stress or depression. Football managers can often fall into this group. Many of the managers that have contributed to the writing of this book have shared mental health challenges that can result in physical and emotional symptoms. Leaders in all walks of life can often neglect their own wellbeing in the constant search for organisational health and concern for the welfare of their colleagues.

The most productive and successful managers or leaders

must work hard to balance their own wellbeing with that of the team, organisation and individuals around them. The National Health Service in England has identified the 'five a day' for mental health as:

1. Connect – Speak and spend time with family, friends and colleagues. These connections need to include reference to the job at hand but also they should involve conversations that relate to life outside of work.

2. Be active – It's easy to become pinned behind a desk and facing a computer screen or a mountain of paperwork that reduces the opportunity for healthy activity. Leaders that balance work and mental health stay healthy through activity.

3. Keep learning – Learning new skills and acquiring knowledge lends itself to a continual sense of achievement and improvement. Micky and I discussed throughout the writing and discussions relating to this book how the research and writing brought us a sense of calm. The additional and diverse learning gave us a sense of inner peace and self-awareness.

4. Give to others – Charity of time and compassion with those close to us helps to build diverse networks and offer a sense of perspective. Many managers and players will visit hospitals and schools to give their

time to others in order to gain a reality and a perspective to their daily lives.

5. Be mindful – Mindfulness or stillness is the concept of being present in the moment. So often in busy lives it can be easy to get frustrated with the past or be concerned about the future. A healthy mental state can focus on the here and now. Sam Allardyce is just one manager who practises meditation to achieve a mindfulness and perspective.

The station will come soon enough

'Over the years I've got better at handling myself away from football,' explains Micky. 'I've learnt to enjoy the day and not worry about the things that might be coming up. It's really important to start working and thinking like this in your first 100 days. You set a pattern then for the future.'

In the build up to the League Two Play-Off Final in 2019, Micky spoke about his mindset. 'It's three days before the game now and I'm not stood in the dugout at Wembley in my head. I'm enjoying this sunny day training with a great group of staff and players. You can't wish your life away thinking about the things that are on the horizon. You've got to savour the moments like these because they don't come around often.

'I am getting better outside of football. I used to go to parties with my wife and I never really wanted to be there. Then I found a way of really enjoying parties. I didn't go there to have fun, I went there to learn! I find someone and

I just learn all about what they do, why they do it and what I can take from the way they do things in their line of work. My wife laughs now and says: 'Who's getting you tonight then?!' Finding out about other people is a great way to expand your mind, understand the challenges and triumphs of others and just 'connect.' Whether it is at a party or with a friend, learning about the world of others can help develop really healthy connections.

This mindset is one which succssful leaders can aspire to. It is captured in the popular Latin phrase of 'carpe diem' ('seize the day') and perhaps most eloquently expressed in the poem by Robert Hastings, 'The Station'. The poem's message is to enjoy life's journey rather than constantly awaiting our arrival at a distant station and it ends with this advisory verse:

> 'So, stop pacing the aisles and counting the miles.
> Instead, climb more mountains, eat more ice cream,
> go barefoot oftener, swim more rivers,
> watch more sunsets, laugh more and cry less.
> Life must be lived as we go along.
> The station will come soon enough'

In every leadership role, the most effective leaders will be the ones who take time to look out of their window and keep a perspective rather than being consumed by a longing for the next stage. For a positive mental state, football managers, school leaders, business executives all need to take more time to enjoy the journey.

'Defeat was like a dagger to the heart'

Sean Dyche is a great example of a manager enjoying his 'five a day'. He portrays a relaxed but confident and focused leader. When we met Sean at the Burnley training ground, he and Micky were in their sportswear after a day on the training pitches of Burnley and Tranmere respectively while I was still in my suit after a day at school, feeling slightly over-dressed! Sean reflected on how he manages his wellbeing. 'I love being with my family. I love the simple things in life like dropping the kids off at school or doing the shopping. The things that my wife finds really dull because she has to do them every day, I love doing it. I also go to the cinema on my own, go to the gym or for a walk in the park. I turn down a lot of media requests, even though they pay.

'When I do them, I donate that money to charity but you have to turn some things down even when your conscience is saying 'do them all'. You've got to give yourself some time to pause, reflect and relax. Going away during an international break was a really tough thing for me. I used to think I should be at the club all the time. Now I do afford myself a day off if I feel I need one or I just want one. I'll go away with my wife or we'll go out for dinner. Just something that's away from football because it is so consuming.'

It was so refreshing to hear a manager of a Premier League club taking his own mental health so seriously. Dyche recognised that if he was not able to take time off, it was unlikely his players and staff would be able to cope with the high demands of their role. 'I read something recently in one of the papers about the Fortune 500 companies looking for people who could switch off. They're doing this because they know that if their leaders can't switch off, they'll burn out and bring that to the workplace. I can switch off now. In the early days, a defeat was like a dagger to the heart and a win was like you'd won the league. With experience, I've learnt how to go out after a game and be ok with it. The pain of a defeat is still there but I can deal with that now. It's so important to be able to do that.'

The importance of friends and family was also discussed as the conversation between the three of us moved on to other matters of emotional intelligence and wellbeing. 'I don't like a fancy lifestyle,' Dyche continued. 'People think you're in the Premier League so you have an exciting life outside of the game. I spend a lot of time on my own on the M6. I travel 50,000 miles a year and that's a lot of time to think.' Micky asked Sean to reflect on his younger self at the outset of his managerial career: 'What would Sean Dyche now say to Sean Dyche at the beginning of his managerial career?' Of all the questions put to him on that Thursday afternoon, this brought the longest pause.

After some deep thought, he replied: 'I think I'd be easier on myself. Give myself more of a break really. I'd also trust [people] earlier. At the beginning of your time, you tend to be wary of everyone. You don't delegate as much because you think you've got to do everything yourself. Now I do and I also accept that I'm an alright person!' Dyche's insight was fascinating. So often, leaders can judge their own self-worth by the results of their team, the football scores or the exam results; the quarterly profits of the business or the success rate of their surgeries. Sean articulated perfectly just how top managers need to be able to manage themselves first.

Be at your BEST

Drew Povey has a distinct model for developing a happy balance alongside the 'five a day'. This is as much about physical wellbeing as it is about mental wellbeing. Drew explained his BEST model to Micky and I over a Zoom call one evening during one of the pandemic lockdowns. 'I've developed a way to cope with the most trying situations which basically relies on the habits you form when the going is good. However, you can just jump onto this model when you are ready to. My BEST model (below) is my routine every morning. Even in my most challenging times, it got me through in good physical and mental shape'.

Drew Povey's BEST Model

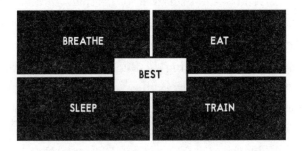

'I make sure I do breathing exercises every day. It helps me to centre myself and get enough oxygen into my system. I try to eat well so I'm putting in the fuel I need for the day,' said Drew. 'Every study stresses the importance of sleep. We need it for all sorts of things. Then I train. I train each morning and have done for over 15 years. Anyone can train, whether it's a walk or a run, whatever you want but something that gets you moving.'

Micky told me that following a play-off final defeat in May 2017, he was in a dark place personally. I asked him, as we spoke to Drew, what he had learnt from that experience and how it had helped him during the lockdown period. 'I learnt a lot about myself then. I learnt that I needed routine. So now I ride my bike for two hours a day. We have a gym in the house so I do an hour in there. I read every day and keep my mind working. All of it means I've got routine so I can cope with almost anything.' He also shared good advice from his wife, Jane. 'At the beginning of lockdown, my wife said, 'We are going to make the most of this. We're going to make this a time of creating memories'. We've even kept a book on it. We planned out what we would do and we've stuck to it.' Whether your adversity is dealing with a worldwide pandemic, a heavy defeat on the pitch or declining sales, getting our five a day using the BEST model and sticking to healthy routines can help us through any storm.

I am certainly a work in progress when it comes to following Drew's 'BEST' model. One of the areas that I struggle with is resting. In my first 100 days, my mind felt hyperactive much of the time. There was a constant stream of ideas, concerns, plans, actions and reflections. There were times when rest felt like a waste of time and the enemy of my productivity. Paul McGee believes that work and rest need not be in opposition to each other. 'I believe that rest is the partner of work. Too many leaders feel a sense of guilt if they are not working flat out. In actual fact, for any elite level sportsperson, rest is an essential part of training. You need to give your brain and body time to recover.'

Paul had another great analogy for this. 'Think of a garden centre that sells hundreds of plants. For each one, there is an instruction card. That card explains what conditions are required for the plant to thrive. Too much work can be like too much sunshine or water. Yes, we need to be dedicated but overworking ourselves is like ignoring that advice card.' Paul continued: 'It is the same when we work with others. Our colleagues, friends or family will thrive in different conditions that we need to try to understand.' In the first 100 days, understanding what conditions our team will thrive within, individually and collectively, is crucial to a successful beginning and continuation of our time as a leader of this group.

In the same vein, overwork can often lead to managers reducing the autonomy of others. Micro-management of a team due to a leader's own insecurities or lack of confidence in others can damage trust within a group. As Paul says: 'Sometimes you need to resign from being the general manager of the universe and accept that others can be trusted to do a good job if they are given the responsibility to. The benefit of this is a shared ownership of a team's successes and defeats. With devolved ownership and leadership, you are building long-term emotional investment in your colleagues.' Such an approach is conducive to a healthier working environment and the formation of a 'team' in its truest sense.

Day 72 – put on your own oxygen mask first

With the 'five a day' notion at the forefront of my thinking, I began to notice the toll that the first 100 days had taken on me. I was exhausted. I was exercising less, working longer hours, putting on weight and working over weekends and throughout the school break. If I were to add up my working hours, I would not be far away from 70 hours a week. I knew that it was not possible to sustain this and continue to think clearly about what needed to be improved in the school. It was also a bad example to set to my colleagues, with whom I spoke a lot about mental and physical health and wellbeing. It was also hypocritical to talk about this with the students and ignore my own advice.

I called on the help of an experienced headteacher who supports fellow headteachers across the country. Patrick Ottley-O'Connor is a fantastic advocate of positive mental health. I invited Patrick into St Bede's on Day 72 and he arrived with his customary smile and purposeful look. I asked if he could share some advice with our leadership team.

He began with a question about our Christmas break. 'How closely did you plan your time off? Did you know when you'd work and when you'd rest?' Patrick asked. We, as a team, looked blankly back at him and shook our heads. He asked us to think about wellbeing as an oxygen mask which might drop down on a plane. 'What advice do they always give you?' he asked. 'Put your own oxygen mask on first,' one of the team replied. Patrick responded by explaining: 'I always start my headships with the first PowerPoint slide of the first meeting showing a picture of my family, with the words: 'Look after yourself before helping others so that together we can make the biggest difference.' That's the oxygen mask analogy in your working life. It's not selfish to look after yourself first so that you can help others.'

Immediately, our leadership team were nodding in agreement and eager to hear more about becoming a more emotionally healthy group. I could not agree more and it was one of the main reasons I wanted to become a head-teacher and a leader of an organisation. I want to work in an environment which values the wellbeing of the community as much as it values the performance of the institution. For me, the two are not mutually exclusive but very much co-dependent for a leader to be successful.

Patrick continued: 'I've been criticised for being too nice. That was probably early on in my headship career and that was because I believe in servant leadership. I am there to help others, not myself. Now I tell my leadership teams that they are 'barrier removal operatives'. It's our jobs as leaders to remove the obstacles that get in the way of high-quality performance.'

'I believe kindness is a superpower'

'For my own wellbeing, I make sure I am conscious of it and I follow my mental health 5-a-day by posting things on Twitter,' says Patrick.

Day 66-79: Managing The Manager

'I'll post my healthy breakfast or my exercise. I then tell my leadership team, colleagues and friends that I'm a leadership supermodel! It's tongue-in-cheek because I'm a bit too heavy and old to be a catwalk supermodel! But I can be a supermodel or a super role model for mental health in the schools I work in. Again, that's not a soft option. If someone is underperforming, I tell them, show them and then support them to get better.'

For Patrick, mental health and wellbeing is not an add-on to what he does. Rather, his zest for his family, his life and his vocation is underpinned and wrapped up in improving the mental health and wellbeing of those around him. He finished by telling me: 'I volunteer my time to help aspiring headteachers, I post videos of my tortoise heading a football (a video that has attracted 2.1 million views!), I document our backpacking holidays and this is all requested by people. I believe in equality which is what I campaign for. I believe kindness is a superpower that I can give to others.' I see this completely in Patrick and I see how this superpower and servant leadership drives everything he does. Whatever your leadership role is, we all have the power to make healthy, happy and productive environments if we serve as leaders, like Patrick does.

From Day 72, we committed to being a healthier leadership team in every respect. If it had not been for this interjection, I believe I would have burnt myself out quite quickly after the first 100 days. The point Sean Dyche and Patrick make is that if managers and leaders do not look after themselves, they cannot be looking after everyone else effectively.

Wellbeing has never been more important as it is today with the impact of COVID-19, raised anxiety levels in general life and for education in particular, a critical problem with teacher retention. Gaining loyalty and long-term commitment from footballers, employees and teachers is an issue for a variety of reasons. A focused wellbeing programme is something that became very important to me following this time with Patrick.

I certainly benefitted from a couple of hours with someone I have come to greatly admire. I have also enjoyed following Patrick's incredible family adventures and thriving home life which he documents on his Twitter page (@ottleyoconnor).

Resilience rebooted

One of the people Micky and I gained a lot of insight from during the process of writing this book was Drew Povey. As mentioned, Drew was the star headteacher from 'Educating Manchester', a hit TV show in the UK telling the tale of a school that rose like a phoenix from the flames after being labelled the worst in Britain. The school performance improved, the £3 million debt was halved, Drew generated a huge amount of income to support the financial recovery of the school and the local community was proud of their local school. However, Drew was then subject to a 'harrowing' investigation in to the running of the school which ultimately led to him resigning. 'I learnt more about resilience during that time than I probably ever will again,' he told us. 'You can deal with things yourself but when it hits your wife and your children – that's tough.'

Drew has gone on to become a nationally renowned leadership coach through his company DP Consultancy. Whether it be business or sport, he supports leaders navigating all manner of challenges.

'We need to rethink our approach to resilience,' he told us. 'It's too easy to use analogies like 'getting up time after time' which can result in a cycle of the same issues happening time and time again. There's a reason we're falling off that bike and if we don't deal with it, we'll keep falling off!'

Drew has a model that leaders of all types can use to manage themselves during challenging times. Drew and I talked this through over the phone as I walked my dog and he sat in his home office. 'For real resilience we need to firstly, **Press Pause**. When we're rock bottom we should reflect on why we are where we are. Secondly, we must **Accept.** This is about accepting that problems will occur and surrendering to this fact. Finally, and this is the key, **Get Curious.** This means asking: 'What can be done differently?'

Povey's Resilience Triangle

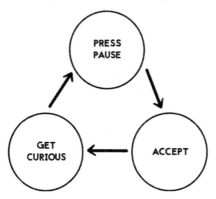

Drew continued: 'We need to accept that to improve our performance and wellbeing, we will need to break ourselves down occasionally. As a leader at Harrop Fold High, I used to get my leadership team to journal. That meant writing about their week, what had gone well and what had not. It made the team think, pause, accept and get curious. It was a bedrock of our success and key to transforming an organisation. It also started some great conversations and kept us all sane!' The passion Drew has for leadership is overwhelming and his clarity of thought, in times of chaos and confusion, is an asset to any football manager or leader when they need to manage themselves.

Preparing the 'Pre-Mortem'

Paul McGee introduced me to the concept of a 'pre-mortem' as we spent hours discussing the notion one afternoon over coffee. 'I prefer to speak to people about responding rather than reacting. That goes for highly-pressurised situations as well. You have to think about the worst case scenario and what you will do,' he said. I gave the example of Micky's brilliant preparation for the play-off final game in which Tranmere had a player sent off after only 58 seconds. Every Tranmere fan at Wembley and around the world that day went into a deep panic! However, the calmest person in that moment was Micky who immediately drew on the 'disaster' scenario planning and adjusted the team accordingly which led to eventual victory.

As Paul highlighted: 'A plan which looks at 'what happens if…' gives you a sense of calmness in the storm because you have an ownership over the situation.' While no-one could have predicted the pandemic that hit the world and UK schools in March 2020, the scenario of having to move to online learning and large numbers of children off school was one which we had discussed previously. My thoughts had been if there was a fire or a flood, rather than a global health crisis. However, the premise was the same in that we were required to teach children remotely. Consequently, our transition could be calm and relatively smooth.

Covid and crisis leadership

However, sometimes even the best 'pre-mortems' or innate resilience cannot solely overcome a crisis outside of our control, such as a worldwide pandemic. Drew is very clear what is required in this situation. 'It's not just crisis management. That's just telling people what to do in times of emergency. The basics. Then, when you've sorted that, you need to start leading. Crisis leadership.'

He continued: 'We learn a lot about ourselves and each other during these times. As John C. Maxwell said, 'A crisis doesn't make us; it reveals us!' During these times we also learn about those immediately around us and the people we work with.' Drew, who works with CEOs of blue-chip companies across the country added: 'I've been working with leaders recently using a new simple framework that I have developed. What I'm trying to do is to help them navigate through the current [COVID-19] crisis and I've given them a simple message to communicate to their teams. The response has been unbelievable and now I think these are three things we need to be telling our teams during periods of crisis.' I eagerly awaited this formula, another model that Drew skilfully constructs to make a leadership principle sound so simple.

Triple-A Crisis Leadership

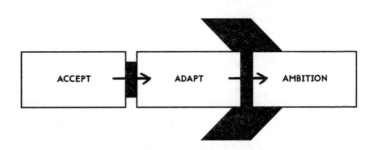

He began with the first step. 'We like to be able to control things. Sometimes we just need to accept the situation. However, as uncertainty increases, our ability to control decreases so our levels of anxiety, worry and fear increase. We need to focus on what we can control. With what you can't control, you have to accept, you've got to give that context that makes the situation understandable.' In a time of crisis, this can be the throbbing worry or concern that can dominate our consciousness.

'Next, you have to adapt,' Drew said, 'There's two key things here in my opinion. We must adapt and shift the way we think about our lives, or our business, probably both! Once that's done we can start to think about the way we'll shift the way we act.'

Finally, and this was the bit I loved, it is all about getting people excited about the future beyond the current state of crisis.

Lancaster's SUMO and 'Hippo Time'

Paul McGee, who is a close friend and Warrington neighbour of Drew, has seen his model of crisis leadership utilised by high-profile sports coaches such as former English international rugby union coach Stuart Lancaster. Paul explained how Lancaster employs his model: 'After matches, Lancaster gets the players to vent and analyse the game. Then they SUMO, they Shut Up about it and Move On to the next challenge.'

Paul went on to explain another stage of deaing with disappointments, which he refers to as having 'Hippo Time'. You need to be able to wallow in the mud after a defeat or a setback. That allows you to process what has happened and arrive at a place of acceptance. Then you SUMO. You own the emotion. You own the feeling. Then you own the fact that it is temporary and that it's not your final destination. Never forget that if you're wallowing for too long, you're setting your thermostat to an uncomfortable level and that can only be negative.'

Both Paul and Drew agree that if you are dealing with crisis, having a view to the future is crucial. Drew explained: 'Our ambition, including aspiration, needs to become really pronounced and powerful once we've got people accepting and adapting. I love the Napoleon quote 'leaders are dealers in hope'. No matter what, keep both your expectations and standards high.' The clarity of Drew's model made me clear about what was required throughout times of real challenge. Of course, as a leader, it's not just you and all too often I forgot who was also affected by my times of challenge and they were the most important people.

It's not all about you!

Sam Allardyce's wife sat patiently as her world famous husband detailed the pressures, sacrifices and personal challenges of football management. At one point during the discussion for this book between Micky and Sam, she asked both men to remember the pressures that leadership brings to the wives of football managers. 'I've had people peering into our house, jumping into our garden and doorstepping us. I've been trapped inside my own home at times. When will you be asking the other halves what the first 100 days are like for them?!'

The point is more than valid. During the first 100 days, a role in leadership can become all-consuming and it can certainly dominate every weekday, evenings and weekends. In my capacity as a school leader, my wife has often remarked that I can be preoccupied and will overreact to issues at home due to the pressures at work. Failure to do so in the first 100 days can lead to family strains that can have incredibly negative implications for those nearest and dearest to leaders in football management – and leaders in general. In the words of my long suffering wife: 'It's not all about you!'

In the world of football, the arduous life of a manager's wife was captured by playwright Peter Tinniswood in 'Dorothy, a Manager's Wife'. The programme aired in October 2000 on Radio 4. It tells the story of a frustrated, disgruntled wife who lives in the shadow of her husband while harbouring resentment toward the almost unfaithful investment her husband devotes to his job.

Most leaders would likely relate to this role, whether they are male or female. Positions of leadership often result in consumption and absorption into the task at hand. In a *Telegraph* article discussing the Tinniswood play, Jim Smith's wife remarks on the sacrifices she has had to make in order to support her husband's career. Talking of moving house on a regular basis, she said: 'One, two, three … seven, eight, nine… 15, 16, 17, including rented … I can sympathise with Dorothy. Sometimes you do get very, very cross. It's been very hard on the children, changing schools, being teased. And the dinner dances, where you find you've lost your husband entirely and sit there on your own. But you get used to it.'

Smith, who managed teams including Blackburn Rovers, Birmingham City, Oxford United, QPR, Newcastle United, Portsmouth and Derby County, moved around more than most. Supportive relationships are the backbone of any successful leader navigating the first 100 days and beyond. Of course, just as the truth may come from the physio room, it will also be likely to come from those closest to us. After all, after the cameras have stopped rolling and another manager is in your dugout, it is the spouse, partner or close friendships that will remain through the peaks and the troughs.

Day 74 – facing some home truths

For me, it all came to a head in a bit of a domestic argument with my wife, Jane, over our dining table. It was essentially a 'who had the most challenging day' competition. Her advice to me was simple. 'You need to learn to switch off and appreciate that those closest to you allow you to have it all. They are the ones often left dealing with the unglamorous, under-valued jobs that are required for a relationship or family to function. If you've taken on all this responsibility, then that's great but you must be able to balance that at home and remember that you need to get off that fast-paced train when you get home. Otherwise, it can have a really negative effect on those closest to you – basically, you need to be around more and, when you are around, we need your undivided attention.'

She was right.

I was falling asleep when the children wanted to play with me. I was grumpy at weekends and not as jovial, purely down to exhaustion. I was throwing my entire emotional self into my first 100 days without a consideration for the needs of my family.

Her words came the day after Patrick had visited St Bede's and following my praise for his advice. I had not, however, taken on board the toll that my first 100 days were taking on my family.

My children were frequently saying 'you're never home' and asking me if I could attend their after-school events. Again, I was in danger of the success of my own 100 days coming at a great cost to my family.

Moving forward I pledged to come home earlier one night a week. I make my wife a cup of tea most mornings before leaving the house. I have taken to putting my mobile phone away when I get in at night in order to avoid checking work emails. I have also added an auto-response to my emails when I am on holiday. All of these actions are an effort to ensure that being an effective headteacher is not at the expense of being a good husband, father and son. I am not there yet. If you asked my wife, she would probably laugh at this chapter and tell me to 'dream on' if I think I've got the balance right. While all leaders make sacrifices, there must be a balance so we don't live to regret the way we are.

As with my wife, the role of the football manager's wife is not one which commands national attention but, without it, the trials and struggles of professional life would be unrewarding and ultimately pointless. A leader of any sphere must remain centred and remember that the ones who care and love us will hopefully be there long after the first 100 days. In order to ensure that happens, prioritising time and listening to loved ones can give a balance to what will be the hardest 100 days in a leader's role.

Support networks

The League Managers Association offers a mentoring programme for all football managers. It is a strong part of their practice which is aimed at offering an impartial view to challenge and support managers in post. It is particularly important for managers setting out on their first managerial role.

The role of mentor with the LMA is to speak with the manager about the pressures of the game. They discuss their approaches to building up team ethics, motivation, the backroom staff but, perhaps most importantly, their own wellbeing.

Mentors are, of course, not limited to football. However, in some professions they can be overlooked as a vitally important aspect of leadership. As a headteacher, my mentor was a national leader of education who heads up an 'outstanding' school nearby. Karen Pomeroy, headteacher of Penwortham Girls' School, offers me counsel but also relates to the challenges I am facing, particularly in my first 100 days. She has been very open with me and shared with me how she has handled high-pressure situations and dealt with stakeholders who have very high standards for the school. In addition, she has spent time walking the corridors with me, noticing my behaviours. It is always useful to have an external view and one which can be trusted to share the psychological and emotional aspects of the job confidentially.

When reflecting on the advice she would give herself now if she was starting her managerial journey again, Shelley Kerr was clear. 'I would make sure I had support. You need to have the right group of people around you. That might include a high performance manager, a sports psychologist and other support networks. It can feel a lonely and isolated job. You shouldn't be afraid to lean on people for support. You can't know everything so you just need to know who does know in some situations.'

Shelley categorises her role as manager into three areas.

'I think that there's management, leadership and being the boss. Sometimes there are times when you just need to be the boss.' The latter point really struck a chord with me and certainly helped me to be able to categorise some difficult conversations or tough decisions into that box. 'Sometimes that can be the hardest challenge because you are making decisions that affect people and their lives. That's tough, it's the toughest part of the job,' she expressed perhaps more openly than in any other discussion we have had during the writing of our book.

Other support networks can include friends who have nothing to do with your profession. It may be that they have no interest in the logistics of your role but they are very concerned about your wellbeing and they are capable of listening well. Often people who are very close to your situation, whether that is a family member, colleague or professional mentor, can have a view affected by their own interests in the time you spend at home, the consequences for them or their perception of your capacity. A completely neutral friend can sometimes be more effective in listening and connecting in a holistic sense rather than one which is purely social or professional.

Where is your physio room?

As well as your own mental health and wellbeing, it's crucial to gain an insight into the wellbeing of those across the team. In the buzz and rush of a normal working day, as leaders we can forget that without this overall sense of positive wellbeing, any actions taken can be undermined.

Micky has a very specific way in which he takes the emotional temperature of the training ground. 'Where is the confessional in your organisation? Where is the place where your players go to tell the truth and share their vulnerabilities, fears and concerns?'

The physio room at Tranmere Rovers when Micky was in charge was where the players would explain how they were feeling, perhaps what was going on outside of football that was affecting them or the internal team dynamics which were impacting upon their performance. 'People are like volcanoes; they have a million things going on below the surface. Occasionally, they'll explode over something. In football it might be a bad pass in training or someone criticising their part in a goal conceded. The further you get into your 100 days, the more you've got to try and understand what is going on below the surface of the players and your staff.

'A lot of the time, you're the boss so they might not come and tell you directly because they're worried you might not pick them to play on Saturday. In a company they might be thinking that you'll overlook them for a promotion. There's so much about mental health these days which is a real plus for our society. The modern leader and manager has to understand something about this and know where your players or colleagues will go to be open and honest.

'People often open up when they are preoccupied with something else so if you can get to hear about that, it can really help you look after your team and get the most out of them.'

Knowing this, Micky makes special time to liaise with the physio and support staff. These crucial members of the leadership team will be more likely to engage in informal and relaxed conversation which may offer valuable insight into the current politics and emotions with the camp. Once known, the manager can address these issues and make sure that, while no action may be required, there is at least an awareness of the subtext to player performance.

Day 76 – Tina provides the thermometer

It was a cold January evening in an Irish pub over a pint of Guinness when Micky and I discussed the physio's room. As ever with our conversations, I began to think about how this applied to my setting at St Bede's. I thought of which member of staff has no real incentive to spin me truth or have a possible agenda either now or in the future.

That's not to say I think other colleagues might lie to me but they may hold back a little because at some point they may be on interview or they may just not feel it appropriate to open up with me. There was one member of staff who jumped to mind, a school librarian, Tina Cain. Her honesty was renowned and her direct nature is abrasively endearing.

On Day 68, having realised this from my conversation with Micky, I went to speak to Tina to talk to her about what she thought we were doing well and what could be better. Very informally, Tina and I carried out a joint TOWS analysis (i.e. Threats, Opportunities, Weaknesses and Strengths). Every organisation may have a character like Tina and if they don't, they should employ one!

Our librarian is a fountain of knowledge when it comes to organisational health. She is the person who teachers and support staff will often have informal conversations with. These conversations may take place while a lesson is progressing, over a coffee during break time or in passing around school. She also speaks with the students and can have a slightly different relationship with them as she is not seen as an authoritarian figure in a conventional school sense. She does, however, command the respect of those who walk into her domain.

When I want to know what the students think about the lunch menu or what our teachers think about a new approach to marking, I know I can ask Tina. She will give no names, betray no confidences, but she will go beyond polite platitudes to tell me what the people around me really think. Such a source of information is invaluable in order to assess the culture of the place so that I can understand the ever-changing environment in which we all work. Tina told me all about a perception that our new students had not quite got into the 'Bede's way of behaving' and that we really ought to do something about that. So assemblies followed after the Christmas break and specific meetings were had with individual students. Tina also shared with me some points and other points that I would act upon.

My 'physio room' is the library. Other 'physio rooms' will be places within the walls of an organisation where informal conversations take place alongside the running of another activity. While the main focus of the individuals is on another matter, physical rehabilitation following injury or helping

11-year-old students to choose reading books, honest conversations take place as walls of caution are inadvertently lowered. During the first 100 days, there will inevitably be walls of caution as a new regime is implemented and a new culture embedded. Things go off track quickly and often irreconcilably if honest viewpoints are not shared in order to benchmark the success of the steps detailed in our earlier chapters.

Levelling out

After the adrenaline-fuelled first 80 or so days, there can be a period of time that is essential to embed the changes that have been brought in to win hearts and minds. This time can make or break the success of the first 100 days. As Micky and I continued our discussions over the phone, dinner and visits to our work places, we arrived at the time to discuss how a manager maintains the changes they have brought in to establish a settled culture. Only when this settled culture is given this time can it support a journey toward success.

We thought of this as a levelling out from a dramatic ascent. The next chapter details Micky's advice to me about maintaining early wins and using this momentum to establish a truly successful, championship-winning team. This advice allowed me to confidently make decisions for the medium to longer-term and so avoid a style of leadership that would overwhelm the team. Crucially, this next chapter allows us to consider how we can maintain a safe intensity to ensure the pace of progress moves from a sprint to a more manageable speed over time.

Reflections

1. What childhood experiences have shaped your personality and character?

2. How will you utilised these experiences to lead and communicate in a manner that is authentic?

3. In what ways will this approach work within the steps outlined in earlier chapters of this book?

4. How will you ensure your family team are in your thoughts and actions during the first 100 days?

5. Will you timetable family time as you timetable you daily life in work?

6. How will you discover your 'blind spots' as a leader?

7. Where is your physio room?

8. How will you ensure you keep your 5-a-day in check?

9. Will you specifically plan for the wellbeing of those close to you?

10. Who are your support networks, personally and professionally?

Chapter Ten

DAY 80-100

 Judgement Day

The course of the journey is set

The first 100 days is much like the take-off of a jumbo jet. The journey to a far destination begins with the preparation of the captain. He reviews the route, the fuel requirements and the weather that lies ahead. Then, as he takes his seat in the cockpit, he works with his time to make the final adjustments to ensure a safe trip which takes into account the obstacles that lie ahead such as adverse weather or strong headwinds.

Once he is ready, he commits to his planned journey by pulling back on the throttle and surging to high speeds, allowing the jumbo jet to leave the ground rapidly and head up into the skies. As the plan angles upward and all are seated, the ride may be bumpy as pockets of air create turbulence and jolts. Through it all, the captain remains focused and calm until the plane has reached its cruising altitude.

At this point, the wings are levelled, the cabin crew rise and the seatbelt sign is switched off. In the same way, the earlier chapters tell the stories of leaders who have propelled their organisation into metaphorical skies through the take-off of the first 100 days. At this point, as the 100 days come to an end, the journey begins. A journey which now has a developing culture and direction. The course is now set and the leader's key role is to maintain the forward momentum as the wings are levelled – to maintain the standards, keep the plan heading in the right direction and remain focused on the journey ahead so that the club, team, department or school can reach its final destination successfully. In order for this to be the case, the leader must adopt a systematic approach.

In-flight service – don't get complacent

The ping, as the seatbelt sign dims, is not a signal that all work stops. Far from it, it is a sign that the work completed before and during take-off now comes to fruition as the plane travels toward its destination.

Indeed, the end of the first 100 days is not a time for complacency. It is, however, a time to allow the fast-paced and often challenging decisions that were earlier made to embed and become the modus operandi of the team. Crucially, this is a time for processes of constant monitoring, reviewing and evaluating.

Micky explained the levelling out phase. 'You get to a point when you've got your systems in place. You've got people understanding the way you work and you have a culture of being successful throughout the building. Then it's time to really practise that Hansei and Kaizen, that day to day self-improvement that you need to have engrained in order to continually improve. Sometimes, I'll stop sessions or meetings if I don't think we're sticking to our principles. I'll tell people that it's not good enough and remind them of the hard work that will have made those first 100 days a massive success. It's the bit that people don't really talk about in leadership books – maintaining and tweaking the standards you've set.'

As with a plane's journey through the skies, the monitoring and reviewing of the journey may require a subtle change to the direction or the altitude at which the plane is travelling at. The speed may be increased or decreased and on occasions – thankfully rarely for an aircraft but more frequently for a football team – emergency action may be required. We will now look at the methods used by the games top managers to monitor and adjust, as appropriate, once the first 100 days comes to an end.

In 'Quiet Leadership', Everton manager Carlo Ancelotti likens this period to the relationship of his leadership arc. That is the time when you, the leader, are now involved with the club and beginning to feel the emotions of the club, like a relationship. Ancelotti describes Pep Guardiola's belief that the arc in football management typically lasts around three years. On this occasion Pep may be optimistic here as Ancelotti explains that the average 'lifespan' of a Premier League manager is less than two years. The figure is actually worse in European leagues such as Spain and Italy.

Therefore, while the first 100 days might be successful, the journey is still likely to be full of turbulence.

Back to Day 1

Just before we returned from the Christmas break, I spoke to Micky about how he would approach returning to a school after the festive holidays. By this point I could predict the answer. 'You've got to stick to the principles that got you the success previously. I hammer them home to the point that even the players are saying the main points. You stick to the plan. Coming back to school or back to a workplace after a break is no different to that.'

So this was my approach. On the first morning back, I reminded the teaching team what our school improvement priorities were. I talked through the things that had gone well and went on to highlight where we knew we needed to improve. This, I stressed, was not just my opinion but their feedback. I spoke about the agreed approaches to behaviour management, staff development and a culture of positive cohesion. I reiterated the plan for the impeding Ofsted visit and the key ways they could support the whole school effort.

What was central to the message, similar to the journey screen available to view for passengers on long haul flights, was a sense of focused travel on our journey toward our vision. It was a reflection back to Day 1. The journey was still the same and we were well on our way towards becoming a 'world class' school. I hoped there would be a sense of accomplishment up to this point and the belief that more was to come. We were heading quickly towards the 100-day marker in fine style. Although, unbeknown to us, our journey and my leadership would be scrutinised earlier than expected.

Managing Cristiano's wellbeing

Like a plane, the atmosphere inside the dressing room is significantly affected by the leader. That atmosphere must be monitored carefully to ensure that the mix of characters with the team are working together effectively.

Writing for LMA Insights, Jeremy Snape of Sporting Edge explains: 'Everyone in the organisation needs to feel that they are able to contribute their own ideas and make their mark, and only then will they truly engage with the team's objectives and take ownership of its results.' Snape goes on to explain how the leader can help each team member succeed as an individual. This may seem counter-intuitive when the focus is on the individual ahead of the team. However, in order for team members to have the will to contribute to a team, they must first feel valued, listened to and respected as an individual.

Micky explains how as a manager he knows his players as individuals. 'I get to know them, the names of their wives, kids and anything else that is important to them. If you want to get the best out of people you have to know what makes people tick and they need to know that you care.' Carlo Ancelotti makes it clear in his aforementioned book that there is no specific chapter on relationships because everything in leadership *is* relationships.

Ancelotti formed tight relationships with some of the highest-profile players in the world, such as Cristiano Ronaldo, Zlatan Ibrahimovic and David Beckham through a quiet, compassionate approach. His approach could be likened to a parent's love for a child. The parent believes in the child and has high expectations that are born out of a genuine love for the child. The job of manager, in its purest form, is one of directing and holding to account. A leader shows the way and takes people with them.

Jeremy Snape makes it clear that leading a group is a real challenge: 'There is only so much you can do to manage the blend of personalities in your organisation, but recruiting on values and character as much as talent can make a big difference. When seeking new talent, think carefully about the mix of people in your team and how new members might enhance or disrupt that dynamic.'

Like the cabin crew who serve drinks and act on behalf of the captain to ensure the wellbeing of the passengers, so a leader must show care and compassion for the members of the team. This is not leadership that lacks the capacity to make unpopular decisions. This is a leadership that takes decisions for the good of the company or team, without forgetting that the players on the pitch or workers at their desks are people rather than pawns in a game.

Day 84 – 'get your boots on'

On Day 84, I began to devise a check-in list to ensure that I was communicating with every member of staff effectively. That evening I caught up with Micky and described these check-ins as 'praise walks'. He was not a fan of this term! He smiled and said: 'You'll annoy me if you use language like that.' With a wry grin, I accepted his point and said: 'Perhaps I'm just walking around and checking people are ok. I'll stick to that rather than getting ahead of myself.'

Whether you have a fancy name like 'praise walks' – clearly not one recommended by Micky – or you use LBWA (Leadership By Walking Around) like Drew Povey or you just walk the aisle, so to speak, and check people are ok, it is an essential part of any journey. Toyota refer to this as *Genchi genbutsu*, also known as 'get your boots on'. Leaders of the most successful car company in the world make sure they go, see and understand.

That walk around on Day 84 highlighted a few issues people were having. It showed me we had a purposeful school with largely happy children that were learning well. We also had, if I needed reminding, an exceptional group of professionals, working hard to improve our school. This day was an important reminder to me that on occasions, it is important to walk around and see the fruits of all of our labour. Where this was not the case, I saw it first hand and began to develop ideas as to what we could be doing to continue our development beyond the first 100 days.

Terry and Lampard call the shots – the trendsetters

For the actions of the first 100 days to be successfully maintained, it is essential that those in the boot room and on the field know exactly what their role is. That is to say, the roles are defined not just in the practical sense but also in a holistic sense. For example, as mentioned in chapter nine, the physio may be the person who holds the most intimate information about the players. That person then needs to feel valued and their input must be clearly respected and sought. The more experienced players in the team need to be clear that they are the trendsetters. They are the ones who will lead by example and set the tone for the other players in the squad. Each member of the team must feel totally responsible for something. A lack of clarity around roles and accountability will quickly become evident through in-fighting, cliques and poor discipline.

Clarity is crucial in defining roles, expectations and methods of accountability. It is also pivotal in defining notions of lines in the sand, non-negotiables or red lines. These boundaries are most effective when they are agreed by the members of the team. It is then simply the leader's job to enforce them.

Carlo Ancelotti is a coach who creates a negotiated set of non-negotiables with his team. Ancelotti speaks with the senior members of the squad and asks them how they would like to be treated. In his book, he describes how he arrived at Chelsea and spoke with key players such as Frank Lampard and John Terry about the time they preferred to train. Ancelotti favoured midday but the senior players preferred 11am in order to have more time in the afternoon. Ancelotti agreed as it did not matter to him. He only saw his job as now enforcing the agreed time in order that high standards of time-keeping could be kept. This was the first step in ensuring that every training session began with a respect for the leader and the team as a whole by being on time. Ancelotti references other successful leaders such as Sir Clive Woodward who also practises such an approach.

This approach is not the only way. On occasion, where the leader sees the need for rapid change, they may need to impose red lines rapidly in order to effect change. Legendary basketball coach John Wooden was a master in the art of effective non-negotiables. In his book, 'Wooden: A Lifetime Of Observations On And Off the Court', he outlines the behaviours he demands such as *fear no opponent but respect every opponent; there is no substitute for hard work; be more interested in character than reputation* – and other wise words. Perhaps his more objective red lines included dress, time-keeping, haircuts and even specific approaches to putting on socks.

Wooden became one of the most revered American coaches of all time due to an approach driven by moral purpose and acute attention to detail. He married vision grounded in a deep faith with a rigorous attention to marginal gains. In both of these regards, he established clarity and consistency in the roles he expected his players and staff to play.

Discretionary efforts – sweep up like the All Blacks

The concept of discretionary effort refers to the effort an individual gives when they are free to choose whether to or not. This is effort beyond the minimum that is expected. When the vision has been shared, the Kaizen culture set, the quick wins achieved and so on, it is then imperative to ensure that discretionary effort is observed and rewarded. That is, to praise the player that goes the 'extra mile'. The player that does this does so through a sense of ownership of their task. They feel a sense of attachment to something greater than their own personal achievement.

In the examples given in this book, the greatest leaders and teams such as Greg Popovich and the All Blacks inspire the individuals within the team to sacrifice their own glory for the collective glory of the group.

A leader might enhance the ownership of a player by asking which part of the team's aspiration most excites them. Leaders drive more discretionary effort when the players feel an alignment to the leadership of the group. Almost always this is based upon strong relationships between the leader and the school, team or organisation. Those in the building feel a connection to the leader and more importantly, they have a sense that the leader cares about them. It is certainly possible, in the short-term, to operate without this although the players in the team will likely only perform to the level that is expected of them. They will not seek to go beyond that. Dan Pink highlights this notion in 'Drive'. Pink cites that only in production lines does a monetary reward serve as a significant motivator for an individual's performance. Rather, people need to be paid fairly and beyond that they need to feel a sense of purpose, mastery and autonomy as described earlier in the book. It is only with advanced discretionary efforts that a team can truly excel.

In 'Legacy', James Kerr details 15 rules that create a wealth of discretionary effort amongst the All Blacks. From sweeping the sheds, senior players cleaning the dressing room after games to player-led disciplinary action, the All Blacks set their own high standards and stick to them. The best players in the world, the best teams in the world and the best leaders in the world exist in a culture of self-motivation and a longing for collective excellence that promote discretionary effort in abundance.

Day 90 – a time and place for praise

From Day 90, I knew I had to put a system in place for praising discretionary effort. This involved a specific time each day when either I or other leaders in the school could praise the efforts of others. We used our morning briefings. We used staff briefings but I also encouraged colleagues to actively seek out opportunities to praise colleagues and students. The mantra of 'catch them doing something well', was especially pertinent for our students.

The positive reinforcement of discretionary effort is easy to forget. It is not deliberate but the more an individual puts effort in, the more it becomes expected. Therefore, a systematic approach to this is helpful to ensure it continually happens. Organisations and teams of any sort must be wary of reinforcing behaviours that do just enough to get by day to day. Where this is the case it can create an apathy. When working with staff that may have lost their passion for the job or their motivation for an immediate task, I think back to Dan Pink's three motivational pillars; mastery, autonomy and purpose. More often than not, one of these pillars may be missing which leads to a drop in discretionary effort.

I realised this system was needed from Day 90 when I saw a dip in the enthusiasm of some colleagues as we entered into the middle of our academic year. The discretionary effort of staff was new when I began but it had become the norm and I had missed a couple of occasions when people had shown great commitment beyond that minimum requirement for their role. The systematic approach I adopted from Day 90 helped me avoid missing that again.

Restarting the engines

It would be wonderful to think that a leader could follow chapters one to nine and ensure success without issue. To believe that this will ever be the case is short-sighted and will only lead to a shock for any leader who may fall into the trap of the 'God complex'. That is a belief that their methods are without reproach and will not at some point need adjustment, realignment or complete overhaul.

After a very successful first 100 days and beyond, Micky and his Tranmere Rovers side narrowly missed out on promotion in his first season. They finished the season with a club record 95 points and broke many other records along the way. Despite this, they lost a play-off final at Wembley, 3-1 to Forest Green Rovers. That defeat was arguably a result of no fewer than eight first team players being injured for the final on a hot May day in London. The following season, Rovers were again hot favourites to gain promotion.

However, by the end of September, Rovers sat 18th in the National League after a home defeat to fierce rivals Wrexham. The defeat was made worse by the fact that the visitors had been down to ten men following a sending off after only 13 minutes.

A chorus of boos greeted the final whistle with the jubilant rival supporters only fuelling the fire of disappointment and anger from the home fans. I asked Micky what his thoughts were about this period and how he 'restarted the engines'. He explained: 'I've been in football a long time. I'm not going to say that didn't hurt or that I wasn't frustrated but I knew we were too good for this to continue. We were making loads of chances and it was actually getting quite embarrassing how many chances we were missing from two yards out, open goals and the like. We didn't panic though and we kept to the principles that we believed in. Of course we combed over why we weren't scoring and some of the goals we were conceding but we didn't shift from our belief in what we were doing.'

Micky outlines an approach which should be adopted in all walks of life that is, when the weather changes in our organisation, it is crucial to make small necessary adjustments but believe in the course that is set and keep going with that direction in mind.

At the end of the 2018-2019 season, Jürgen Klopp's Liverpool achieved a record points haul in the Premier League yet still lost out on the title to Manchester City on the final day. During that summer, there was overwhelming pressure from fans to make big money purchases to enable the Reds to take that extra step and win the prize that had eluded them for so long. Yet Klopp resisted the temptation of the transfer market and made only minor tweaks to his playing squad – with the result that his team landed the Premier League title a season later after setting yet another record points haul.

Post-success trauma and going again

Micky also had a fascinating insight into life after great success. 'You can actually have a low after a great victory. It's not something that you might talk about as a leader but I've felt it after big games like the League Two Play-Off

Final win in 2019. I was mentally prepared for both victory and defeat so I actually felt really calm afterwards. After that [winning] goal went in, that really completed our objective at Tranmere, to get them back into League One and I had a feeling that must be like a very mild form of post-traumatic stress. You go through a season of 50-plus games with highs, lows and everything in between. You've got the hopes and dreams of thousands of people in your hands, to an extent. If you're leader of a business your success still affects colleagues, their families and shareholders. In schools you've got children, parents etc. In leadership roles, the after-effects of successfully completing your objective or mission can be surprisingly hollow.

'As a leader, you've got to experience that and then prepare for it the next time around. After we had achieved incredible back-to-back promotions, I felt a bit numb but again it's just another facet of leadership that you've got to prepare for and deal with. The end of the first 100 days, completing that rapid ascent, can leave you with a similar emotion.

'You've got to take that moment to take it all in and reset yourself to go again. Going back to the chimp model earlier in the book, the chimp might be hammering around wanting more adrenaline but it might not be there immediately. For me, you've got to go back to being in the moment, whether that's mindfulness or whatever you want to call it, remember that the quiet times are part of your journey as well.'

Going back to Liverpool Football Club, their unrivalled success during the 1970s and 1980s was built on not resting on theur laurels. They would celebrate their success but the planning for the next triumph would start immediately. That is a key hallmark of any great side that reaches the top and aspires to stay there. The biggest success for any elite team will always be 'the next one'.

The key to further growth – IQ v EQ

In terms of continuing to develop as a leader during and following the first 100 days, Mark Palios noticed a decisive factor in his years as senior partner at Pricewaterhouse-Coopers. As we discussed continuing the momentum of the first 100 days, Palios explained: 'We had the best of the best in the city. I'd see guys that had done really well up to the age of 26 or 27 but all of a sudden a lot would hit a ceiling. It dawned on me that they'd reached their premium of time. What I mean by that is that there were simply no more hours in the day they could work. IQ [Intelligence Quotient] is the order qualifier but EQ [Emotional Quotient] is the order winner. I could get IQ as a commodity, first-class degrees from Oxford – commodity but not EQ. These guys that hit the ceiling had the IQ, they had the best degrees from the best universities, that was the order qualifier, that got you in the door. You have to have the EQ to be able to work through people.'

Palios went on to describe how this related to his vision for the ideal manager. He described him as 'hardworking, having high EQ … reflective and someone able to bring a group of people together. The average fan can pick out a good player but it takes a manager with high EQ to be able to bring that group together. Your manager needs to be able to bring out the best in players and team spirit.' The similarities with any leadership role were clear, whether it was leading a team of directors at PWC or a football club. While IQ might offer an individual the chance of a leadership role, it is the EQ that determines how far they can lead their team. An advanced EQ allows the leaders to understand their team in order to reflect upon the correct approach for the team and for the individuals within that team.

Like Palios highlighted, individuals can rise through the ranks for being effective in their particular field while they are the ones making the decisions, taking action and driving progress forward themselves. The most successful leaders will continue this growth when they can inspire, direct and support others so that, as Palios stated, 'it's all about the institution, not the individual'.

You're just part of a bigger journey – perspective

This sentiment was shared by Micky who explained to Palios and I how his understanding of the role he occupied has evolved over his 550-plus games in management ranging from Fleetwood Town to Dundee United. 'In my early days, it was all about me. I used to think that every game was about me and I was the one who would start and finish the journey of team. Now I look at it and I think about what my part is in the journey of this club.

'When I was at Shrewsbury, I had just left Barnsley and spoke to the chairman. He told me that there was no money, no training ground, we were about to sell some top players. They had just been relegated and I think we only had about four players. By the time I finished, we had been promoted, we had plenty of money in the bank and we had a new shiny training ground. I never got the benefit of that work but the next man did. They went on to get to the play-off final and had these fantastic facilities.

'At Tranmere, it was the other way around. I got the benefit of Gary Brabin's work (Micky's predecessor). I took over a team that just needed a wee bit of cajoling, the training ground was on the way and I even got his car! I think if I was looking at a job now, I'd be saying that I might not be the man who finishes this job. I might be the person who takes it from A to B, but not to C, D and so on. You need to understand that you're on this journey. It is the same with the players. I might not get the benefit of these players if it is a development project. Part of the job as a manager is that you're part of the journey and like you say, (referring to Palios), it's the institution not the individual.'

The message here allowed me to reflect on my own role. In fact, whatever capacity a leader is working within, that sentiment shared by Micky and Mark Palios can be crucial to keep a perspective on the job we do as leaders. We are part of a journey. What we must recognise as leaders is what part of the journey we are in. Then we have to act accordingly to retain an honesty about the decisions we make for the long-term benefit of the organisations we lead and the people we serve who will follow us.

Understanding this has given me a great deal of additional clarity and a degree of calmness about the actions I was taking as we reached the 100-day mark. There will always be a limitless number of improvements a leader can make. What these three hours with Mark and Micky taught me is that we must prioritise effectively to suit internal and external agendas. These decisions need to be communicated effectively internally and externally to maintain credibility. Finally, as our leadership tenure continues, understanding our part in the journey is key with a central mantra of the institution and not the individual to keep us focused and grounded.

Ole's 100 per cent control on Day 100

On March 28th, 2019, exactly 100 days since Executive Vice-Chairman Ed Woodward approached Ole Gunnar Solskjær to take temporary charge of the team, he was given the full-time managerial job at Manchester United.

Speaking to the club's communications department, Ole said: 'From the first day I arrived, I felt at home at this special club.' He added: 'It was an honour to be a Manchester United player and then to start my coaching career here. The last few months have been a fantastic experience and I want to thank all of the coaches, players and staff for the work we've done so far. This is the job that I always dreamed of doing and I'm beyond excited to have the chance to lead the club long-term and hopefully deliver the continued success that our amazing fans deserve.'

In the same article, Woodward highlighted that Ole's achievements in his first 100 days went beyond simply improving results on the pitch. He said: 'Ole brings a wealth of experience, both as a player and as a coach, coupled with a desire to give young players their chance and a deep understanding of the culture of the club. This all means that he is the right person to take Manchester United forward.'

He continued: 'I want to thank Ole and the coaching team for everything they have done so far and congratulate him on this richly deserved appointment. The fans and everyone at the club are behind him as he looks to take us where we need to be and build the next stage of our history.'

That last sentence highlighted Ole's efforts, with the support of Mick Phelan, in unifying a disjointed culture and bringing about a great hope for the future. As I am sure you can appreciate from getting to know Ole and Mick throughout this book, they knew their work was not finished. In fact, they both realised that it was just beginning.

Ole told us: 'Now we could go about changing things. Now we knew we were here permanently we could start making those plans that you know will help bring about the new adventure for Manchester United that we all want to be a part of.'

As we drew our afternoon together with the duo to a close, Micky closed by saying: 'As a first 100 days goes, you two smashed it by the way! You might feel honoured that United chose you. But they should be thanking their lucky stars that you chose them.'

And that is where we will leave Ole and Mick. Theirs is a text book case study of a successful first 100 days. They both realigned and turned around the culture of one of the most famous football clubs in the world. They had balanced EQ and IQ. They had managed the take-off and anticipated the turbulence before moving into a cruising altitude where they began to impact every aspect of this great club.

Day 100

Celebrating our 100th day of this journey was a very cathartic occasions. Micky and I sat with Andy Hodgen and Michael Kinsella in a Brazilian restaurant. We reflected back on a journey that we had enjoyed. Micky believed it had been a positive one for him. 'I've improved as a manager through this. I admire how patient you have to be as a headteacher. I've had to think about the way I do things in a different way. I think I'm calmer because I know what I'm doing now, I understand it. I'll read this book and remember what we've discussed. I will be able to look back and pick up each chapter when I need it, like a manual.'

Micky and I agreed over that Brazilian feast that there are no guarantees of success but we were both in agreement that following the blueprint laid out in this book will give football managers and leaders in all walks of life the best chance of getting where they want to be.

Fundamentally, I believe that the first 100 days depends on that triangle of position, people, processes and now, heading towards and beyond 100 days, persistence. I would argue that getting to grips with each one of these aspects in order can give you a provisional flight path. In this book, the beginning looks at understanding the position; the middle focusses on the people and the latter chapters focus on processes. This is the flight path that leads you to this final chapter, this final 'P', persistence.

Day 80-100: Judgement Day

Step Model For A Successful 100 Days

PERSISTENCE
Maintaining speed, direction and focus after the intial ascent

PROCESSES
Leadership, team talks and managing yourself

PEOPLE
Vision, wins, players, culture and leadership

POSITION
Where is the organisation at (STARS model)

At St Bede's, as at Tranmere during Micky's first 100 days, there had been highs and lows. However, I developed a great internal resilience to trust the principles of my approach. Micky echoed this and said that he now had a better understanding of why he did what he did. We both left this process with a clarity about the steps we took, in the words of Micky, 'to give ourselves the best chance of winning'.

Judgement Day

For Micky and I, the culmination of the work did not arrive at 100 days, although these first days set the tone for future success. Ironically, for both of us, our judgement days arrived in May 2019.

For me, it was May 8th, my wife's birthday, VE Day and also the day that St Bede's was inspected by Ofsted. Like a football final, this is a one-off event and not the sole indicator of a successful 100 days. However, like a cup final or crucial title decider, these occasions are significant in deciding how we are remembered as leaders and they dictate, in the eyes of many, how successful our tenures have been.

So, on May 8th, Ofsted arrived. May 8th would actually be around Day 175 for me but the work done in the first 100 days was key in achieving a successful day. The report would identify an 'open and friendly' culture and one which had 'high expectations'. The official report pointed to the school's leadership being a 'clear strength'. Most pleasingly, this leadership was recognised as being devolved and prevalent throughout the school. One of the first people I contacted to share our success with was Micky. His input and mentoring supported me throughout my first 100 days and helped the school to secure a report that all of our staff should be very proud of.

For Micky, his judgement days began with the League Two play-off semi-finals against Forest Green Rovers. The first game was a tightly-fought affair. The away side had a man sent off early on. Tranmere were then held to a 1-0 victory. There was a steely experience to Micky's after-match reaction. While the Forest Green manager celebrated with the away supporters – as if they had set themselves up to win on the return leg – Micky was calm and readied the club for the return leg.

Prior to the kick-off of that second game, Micky refused to talk about the final the week after. The Forest Green manager, however, talked about his hopes of making it to Wembley. Both managers were experienced and successful in situations such as this. Yet Micky appeared to have an absolute focus on the task at hand. The rivalry between the two sides was fierce and there was a danger that emotions could negatively affect either side.

Day 80-100: Judgement Day

As it turned out, Tranmere ran out victorious over the two games. The next step, the next judgement day, was a trip to Wembley for the League Two play-off final.

In a tense affair, the game went to extra time after a goalless 90 minutes. Before the final, the team had decided on a low key build-up. They had discussed how to prepare collectively. There were leaders all over the pitch. There was a resilience that had been built up through the ups and downs of the season. Ultimately, Tranmere stuck to their principles of play. They did not panic or become flustered. This led to a last-minute winner and jubilant scenes as Rovers secured their place in League One. Micky became a back-to-back promotion-winning manager, a rare feat. All season, Micky had used his knowledge of the position and the people to develop processes to set the club up for victory. From there, the focus was persistence, maintaining high standards and striving toward a shared goal.

The end of our professional journey, in the year we wrote this book together, was a very successful Ofsted inspection for me and a promotion winning season for Micky. All of which would not have been achievable without a first 100 days that propelled our leadership toward success.

The journey is far from over. The destination has not been reached.

After the first 100 days, there will be many more days to follow. When new challenges arrive, we will both use our learning from the writing of this book to start our ascent again.

We hope you will too.

Reflections

1. *How well do you know your team?*

2. *What methods will you use to check in with them?*

3. *When will you actively seek to ensure they know their individual value and importance?*

4. *How will you reinforce the values laid down in the first 100 days?*

5. *Is your backroom team and playing staff clear on their roles and responsibilities?*

6. *How will you define and reinforce your non-negotiables?*

7. *What ways will you promote discretionary effort?*

8. *How will you actively rejuvenate your team?*

9. *What are you key learning points from the last 100 days?*

10. *How will your learning from this book and your wider experiences influence your next 100 days?*

HOW HAS THIS 100 DAY JOURNEY HELPED YOU?

After beginning from a chance meeting in a gym on a warm August morning, Micky and I sat with Drew Povey at Tranmere's training ground on the Wirral.

We had come together to reflect on the experiences we had enjoyed over the last two years, especially during those first 100 days. I had asked Drew to come along so that he could offer his insight and draw out the key learning points from this incredible journey.

We hope that you will have your own learning points as you reach this reflective chapter. Here are ours.

How has writing this book changed you?

Phil: This book was an exploration into what it takes to lead a team with passion, clarity and calmness. There is no doubt in my mind that I fulfil my role as a headteacher very differently because of this experience. I believe that I have a lot more confidence in myself and a much greater courage in my convictions.

Micky: It's been great to see you grow, mate. When I first met Phil, he wasn't as confident in himself. He didn't believe in himself as much as people might think. He underestimated what he was capable of. Phil always thought someone else had a better way of doing things. I challenged him to say 'be you and trust you'. I've seen you become yourself and your school has become a representation of you. Your school is you and my team is me. You used to be all about procedure but now you're you. It's been great to see you grow.

Drew said: You've completely changed [Phil]. You used to ask me a lot. You used to talk to me about what Micky has told you. It's not that you've stopped doing that but now you're telling me what you're doing and you've a confidence in yourself which is great to see.

What have you learnt about yourself?

Micky: This process had made a better manager. I am much calmer now and I don't react to things emotionally. I think, 'what am I here to do?' then I'll approach things in a way that I believe will make my team, the players and the situation better.

Drew: It's a lot like what we talked about before, it's a process of learn, then unlearn and then relearn. It is the way we evolve as leaders over the course of a season, a financial year or even just in our daily lives.

Micky: Absolutely. It is just having clarity in why you're doing or saying what you are. Before writing this book, I would do things because it just seemed the right thing to do. Perhaps when things weren't going well, I wouldn't know exactly why but now I understand the people and the process so I just get it more.

I never realised how important culture was and language. I consciously use my language now to connect with a culture and the people in it. You have to help educate them, like you guys do in a classroom, so that they understand the way you're behaving and why. That's been my biggest improvement I would say as a manager, I understand culture much more now. I didn't see that it was that important. Now I see that getting the right person for the right job, at the right time, for the right culture, is a must. If you attack a culture, then you're only going to come undone. You've got to shape and mould it so that gradually over time it becomes what you want it to be. I can see that Phil's school now reflects him as a person and it's a personification of him. Like Sean Dyche at Burnley. Or Joe Royle at Oldham and Everton.

The whole journey has helped me learn a lot about me and what has made me the way I am. I never thought it would do that. I think everyone should do something like this to pause and reflect.

I've learnt the value of what my mam and dad taught me when I was growing up. I've seen the values they gave me and understood how I apply that to the way I run my football team and go about my life. Those are values like: be a good guy, accept fate sometimes and that 'what's for you won't go by you'. That last thing was something my mam always said. I heard an old lady from Glasgow say it on the news the other day and I fell about laughing. I hear myself saying that in my head more now. This learning has made me more comfortable in myself. I've got my ideal job but if it went tomorrow, I'd be fine. I could go on to another job, another role or walk away from the game completely if I felt that was the right thing to do. I'm a lot clearer and calmer about things in my head now. I used to think it was all about me but now I accept that there are things I can control and things I can't. Both of which I can accept now. That's come from really looking at leadership and personalities.

Phil: For me, it has been a privilege to be a part of this personal and professional exploration for Micky. I felt I have gained just as much. I have grown in confidence and assurance after seeing a variety of leaders operate in their own unique ways.

From my parents, too, I have taken calmness and a resilience that no matter what may happen, it can be overcome. My parents are not involved with football in any way but the way they don't get too excited in good times or sad in hard times has clearly resonated with my persona. They also exude a kindness to others which is authentic and creates a sense of trust amongst their friends and peers. With both of my parents being born and raised in Birkenhead, the home of Tranmere, much of the qualities that the area has are, I hope, reflected in my own character.

So often I have changed my approach to an issue because

of my learning in this book. The day of this meeting, I had received quite an abrupt and condescending email from an experienced member of staff regarding an issue around standards across the school.

Perhaps two years previously, I would have either ignored it to show my annoyance or I would have challenged the tone of the email.

Now, however, I am grateful for it. By not reacting emotionally, taking a step back and realising that this member of staff actually cares about the school's standards, I responded differently. I actually went back to the member of staff and thanked them for their candour and for caring so deeply about this school's performance. As you might expect, they were taken aback but then we had a really productive discussion which led to their continued support, positive action to address their issue and a continued team ethic modelled by both of us.

Furthermore, I learnt there was not an off-the-shelf formula [to be a leader] but rather key attributes that I could control and develop to give myself the best chance of being successful in my chosen field of leadership.

As I stand back with the words on the pages and the recordings as a log of these lessons, I see a wealth of experience that no qualification could offer. Having read through the pages of this book, we hope that the readers will appreciate the lessons they have gained from parents or those who have supported their development.

We also hope that they will see that, despite the footballing glory of the managers we met, they have been successful because of human traits rather than any genius gene. To be yourself is the biggest challenge you might face.

How can this book help people in football?

Phil: Whether they be playing or managing in Sunday league, amateur, semi-professional or in the professional ranks, I hope people see a way of giving themselves every chance of being successful. I also hope that it gives these managers a belief that they can could manage as well as the top people because they understand the principles. There is a lot of research in education that says most children will have high aspirations, it is often the experience, or lack of it, of being around people who have achieved their aspirations which can determine whether dreams are realised.

Micky: There's never been a book written about what to expect coming into this job and so many go into it unskilled and not ready. So much comes at you straight away but they haven't thought about it. The book gives you a thought process of what you're about to face. Rather than the door opens and it's a tsunami [of challenges]. On top of that, you've got to win games of football. I hope it gives people a bit of a plan so that ultimately, they don't get the sack!

Drew: Wouldn't it be great if every owner of every football club, business owners and chairs of governors in schools read this book. I see it so often in the corporate world that people are not sure which leaders they want and why. Football owners often won't know what the manager actually does. So, if they don't understand that, how can they make the right decision for their clubs?

How do you hope this book will help people in business?

Phil: I believe that business leaders can learn a great deal from the examples set by top football managers. As we have found through our meetings with the figures included in this book and our observations from our armchairs of managers going through their first 100 days, there is no hiding place in football.

In business, there may be time to settle in, prepare and evaluate. In fact, you can have a rough first quarter or poor first academic year, yet still be there for a period of time after that before you are judged on your performance. Moreover, in most cases, the stakeholders will be patient and understanding. It would seem outrageous in any other walk of life for a leader to be judged within a matter of weeks, sometimes even days, when they have to deal with an inherited team, limited time and limited resources. However, in football, if those first few days and weeks are not a success, the heat is already on.

I hope that the world of business will take greater heed of those first few days in order to have a big impact within the first 100 days. That might not mean making significant decisions but it will mean quickly evaluating the situation and immediately adapting and adjusting priorities and actions to suit.

Micky: I originally agreed to do this book because I believe business underestimates how good managers are. When I've got more into this, I think a lot of managers don't really know what they do, they just do it from instinct. Probably only a couple had a real business mind. I want business to learn from this and how we deal with culture, emotion and everything.

I really think everything is about culture and managers have to be experts at this. Motivation, inspiration and recruitment are all about culture. The good ones survive because they've got their culture.

When the chaos is on, you stay in your culture and you believe in your behaviours. The manners and the soft skills, you need to keep all of them.

How do you hope this book will help people in life?

Micky: I hope this book does the same thing for others that it has done for me in my life. I've got to know myself better. It has given me a route to do that. I wouldn't have known about that before.

For instance, I've thought about what my values are. I've thought about why things like timekeeping are so important to me. I've actually delved back into my past and challenged my thoughts on this. Like when my mam said, 'Don't speak to anyone like you wouldn't like to be spoken to yourself.' I've brought this into this building. We have that as a value here now.

I told a player, who had an anger issue: 'Count to 10 and

if you still feel like that at three or four then say it or do it.' That was a message from my mam and I remembered that. It's things like that, this book has really made me think back to my childhood and question why am I the way I am.

Phil: If you are kind, positive and show trust, you will draw people to you that want the same things. Of course, there needs to be a technical knowledge which must be used to improve systems and processes. However, in terms of leadership, I am very clear on the approach that I believe will have sustained success for the first 100 days and beyond.

In my opinion, whether you're leading a Premier League team or your family, there are three key principles I hope this book reinforces throughout: 1. Be authentic and kind. 2. Have a plan and work hard at it. 3. Look after yourself and those around you. I think showing my children John, Betsy and Rory that example will always be my ultimate goal.

Coming full circle

When Micky, Drew and I met on the training ground to discuss our book journey, the news had just broken that the League One season had been suspended due to the COVID-19 pandemic.

At the time, we were unaware that this would be Micky's last day at Tranmere's training ground. Later, during the first national lockdown, he would be offered the chance to manage a Scottish Premiership side.

Micky was appointed as the new boss of Dundee United on July 6, 2020. This was the break that Micky had worked for and that his great track record deserved. He would be fulfilling a lifelong dream of managing in his native Scotland.

Following his appointment, the Scottish media began to dig in to his illustrious career and they highlighted a record of success which is amongst the best in lower league English football. Now, Micky was no longer a 'lower league' manager. It was a title that I always felt did not do his ability justice, now he was a Scottish Premier League manager.

Having written this book together, Micky knew exactly what he had to do to get his first 100 days off to the best possible beginning. 'I knew I needed to get my homework done before I started because I was a fairly late appointment. I only had three weeks to get the lads ready for their first game back in the SPL. Many of them hadn't played in the division before and half the squad were very young,' Micky told me. 'I've known the Sporting Director for many years. He's a pal of mine so we could be really honest about where the club was at. I had a good chat with the owners and saw how they operated. I liked what they had to say and I saw that they were ambitious but realistic, which is what you need.

'I then got to know this town and this club. I used to pretend I was a Dundee United player when I was a boy. I knew all about the history of the club and what a magnificent support base they have. I got really excited about living and working here. Like I've said before, it's like starting a new relationship.' And so the journey begins again…

The following people were personally interviewed by Phil and Micky during the writing of this book:

Ole Gunnar Solskjær

Ole Gunnar Solskjær is a modern-day legend at Manchester United, success he is now trying to emulate as manager at the club. The Norwegian moved to England as an unheralded striker in 1996 but was then a key member of the United squad, winning the Premier League six times, the FA Cup twice and, most famously, netting the winning goal in the 1999 Champions League final, a last-gasp goal that cemented his place in United folklore. As a manager, Solskjær returned to Norway, and Molde, in 2010 to embark on his managerial career and after domestic success, he spent a short spell in charge of Cardiff City before returning for a second spell at Molde in 2015. United appointed Solskjær as caretaker manager in 2018 and after winning 14 of his first 19 matches, he was given the job full-time in March 2019.

Sam Allardyce

After a two-decade long playing career, Sam Allardyce's first job in football management was with Irish club Limerick in 1991 before joining Preston North End in 1992. Since then, his peripatetic career has taken him across the English leagues and across the country. Spells at Blackpool and Notts County, where he won the then Third Division in 1998, were followed with seven and a half years at Bolton Wanderers who he guided to the Premier League in 2001 and established them as a consistent top-flight force.

Allardyce has managed a record eight Premier League clubs – Bolton Wanderers, Newcastle United, Blackburn Rovers, West Ham United, Sunderland, Crystal Palace, Everton and, currently, West Bromwich Albion – as well as enjoying a short spell as the England national manager.

David Moyes

David Moyes has managed more than 500 matches in the Premier League and is renowned as one of the most astute thinkers in the game. A three-time winner of the prestigious League Managers Association Manager of the Year award, he rose to managerial prominence at Preston North End, helping them gain promotion to the Championship in 2000 and only narrowly missing out on promotion to the Premier League the following season. He became Everton boss in March 2002 and spent over 11 years at Goodison Park, transforming Everton's fortunes on a very limited budget. Moyes was chosen as Sir Alex Ferguson's successor at Manchester United in 2013 but left after 10 months in the job. Spells at Real Sociedad and Sunderland followed and Moyes is currently in his second spell in charge of West Ham United.

Sean Dyche

Sean Dyche holds the distinction of being the longest serving manager in the Premier League, having been appointed Burnley boss in 2012. Since then, he has consolidated the Lancashire club's position in the top flight and turned Burnley into one of the most effective and hard-to-beat sides in English football. Dyche's playing career involved spells at seven clubs, including Nottingham Forest and Watford, and he was appointed Watford manager in 2011 before leaving at the end of the 2012 season. Burnley saw their opportunity and installed Dyche at Turf Moor, where he has become one of the most popular managers in English football.

Mark Palios

Mark Palios is a rarity in the English game – a former player who has become a team owner. Alongside wife Nicola, Palios owns Tranmere Rovers; a team he used to play for. When his playing career came to an end after spells at Prenton Park, Crewe Alexandra and Southport, Palios became a chartered accountant and was named as the Football Association's Chief Executive in 2003. After leaving The FA, Palios continued to develop his interests in the administation and business side of sport, and football in particular, before taking a controlling interest in Tranmere in August 2014.

Joe Royle

A former striker for Everton, Manchester City, Bristol City and Norwich City, Royle scored 154 goals during a career that saw him capped six times for England. As manager, he led Oldham Athletic to the First Division as champions of the second tier in 1991. Oldham also reached the 1990 League Cup final and the last four of the FA Cup on two occasions. Royle later took charge of Everton, guiding them to a famous FA Cup win over Manchester United in 1995. He also managed Manchester City and Ipswich Town.

Shelley Kerr

Kerr enjoyed a highly successful career with clubs including Kilmarnock, Hibernian and Spartans and played 59 times for Scotland as a talented and tough defender. Throughout her playing career, Kerr demonstrated a desire to coach and has managed a wide array of sides including Spartans, Arsenal and the Scottish national side. She won the FA Women's Cup with Arsenal in 2013 and 2014 and when she later became the manager of University of Stirling men's first team in 2014, she became the first woman in Britain to manager a senior men's team. She was awarded an MBE in the Queen's 2018 Birthday Honours for services to football.

Drew Povey

A self-confessed leadership geek, there is little that Drew Povey has not read about regarding leadership. Povey now has his own consultancy firm following his time as a leader in sport and education. His leadership in education has drawn national acclaim following the Educating Manchester series. Along the way, Povey has had to deal with great highs, incredible lows and everything in between. Through it all, he has developed user-friendly leadership models and approaches which have proved popular and effective.

Paul McGee

Author Paul McGee has written 13 books which help people across the globe to manage themselves in a positive manner. His words in this book will help any leader to have a great perspective on the challenge at hand.

Contributor Profiles

Tuesday Humby

Tuesday is headteacher at Ormiston in Widnes, Halton, and a Teacher of Law, Politics and Drama. Before her arrival the school previously had a dire reputation – the roll was falling and it had been rated 'inadequate'. Her school is now judged 'outstanding' and ranked in the top 100 in the UK. She is a winner of the Varkey Foundation Global Teacher Prize, awarded for changing lives through education.

Patrick Ottley-O'Connor

Patrick has been a headteacher for 17 years. The current head of Westhoughton High School in Bolton, the former executive principal of North Liverpool Academy is a well-known figure on social media where he advises followers on collaborative leadership and wellbeing.

The First 100 Days Bibliography:

Bennis, Warren; Nanus, Burt (1985). Leaders: Strategies for Taking Charge, Harper and Row, New York, USA
Watkins, Michael (2009), Picking the Right Transition Strategy, Harvard Business Review (Online: https://hbr.org/2009/01/picking-the-right-transition-strategy)
Collins, J (2001), 'Good to Great', Random House, London
Beveridge, H & Hunt-Davies, B (2011), Will it make the Boat Go Faster', Matador, London, UK
Covey, S, (1989), The 7 Habits of Highly Effective People, Simon & Schuster UK Limited, UK
Lombardi Jr., V (2003), 'The Lombardi Rules', McGraw-Hill Professional Education, USA
Sinek, S (2009), 'Start with Why', Penguin, London, UK
J Jenas, (Sept 2017), 'Palace need to stick to what they're good at'
Available at: https://www.bbc.co.uk/programmes/p05fthqh, [Accessed 09/09/2018]
Maxwell, John C (2019), 'Leadershift: The 11 Essential Changes Every Leader Must Embrace', Harper Collins, New York, USA
Steiner, C, (1974), 'Scripts People Live', Grove Press, New York, USA
Rogers, Everett M. (1962). Diffusion of Innovations, Glencoe: Free Press
Critchley M, 'David Moyes prepared to make his West Ham players cry in order to avoid Premier League relegation', The Independent (8th November, 2017).
Liker, J, (2004), 'The Toyota Way', McGraw-Hill, New York, USA

The First 100 Days

Ferguson A, with Moritz, M (2015), Leading, Hodder & Stoughton, UK
Collins, J (2001), 'Good to Great', Random House Group Limited, London, UK
Pink, D (2009), 'Drive', Penguin, New York, USA
Jansen, C (2011), 'Quaternity: The Home of Claes Jansen', Available online: http://www.claesjanssen.com/index.shtml, [Accessed: 01/11/2018]
Kotter, J.P. (1996), 'Leading Change', Harvard Business School Press, USA
Beveridge, H. & Hunt-Davis, B (2011), 'Will it make the boat go faster?', Matador, Leicester, UK
Barrett, R (2013), 'Building a Values-Drive Organisation, Routledge, New York, USA
Lencioni, P, 'The Five Dysfunctions of a Team', Jossey-Bass, San Francisco, CA, USA
Redknapp, H, 'A man walks on to a pitch: Stories from a life in football', Ebury Publishing, London, UK
Crellin, M (2017), 'Gareth Southgate wants to create an England leadership group', Sky Sports, Available online: https://www.skysports.com/football/news/12016/10804313/gareth-southgate-wants-to-create-an-england-leadership-group [Accessed: 06/06/2018]
https://www.businessleader.co.uk/seven-leadership-lessons-learned-from-gareth-southgate/47811/
Mujis, D, Quigley, A and Stringer, E (2018), 'Metacognition and Self-Regulated Learning', Education Endowment Fund, London, UK
Hart, S (2015), 'Leicester City in their own words: Jamie Vardy, Claudio Ranieri and more on why the Foxes are flying high', Online at: https://www.independent.co.uk/sport/football/premier-league/leicester-city-in-their-own-words-jamie-vardy-claudio-ranieri-and-more-on-why-the-foxes-are-flying-a6771036.html, [Accessed: 08/05/2018]
Lamont, T (February, 2010), 'The half-time talk: football's final mystery', Online: https://www.theguardian.com/sport/2010/feb/07/team-talks-football-managers, [Accessed: 09/10/2018]
Khaneman, D (2012), 'Thinking Fast and Slow', Penguin, London, UK
McGee, P (2005), 'S.U.M.O (Shut Up, Move On): The Straight-Talking Guide to Succeeding in Life', John Wiley & Sons, London, UK
Coyle, D (2018), 'The Culture Code', Penguin, London, UK
Ancelotti, C, Brady C & Forde, M (2016), 'Quiet Leadership', Penguin, London, UK
Covey, S (1999), 'The 7 Habits of Highly Effective People', Simon and Schuster, UK
Brown, B (2018), 'Dare to Lead', Penguin, London, UK
Rogers, C, Smith, T, & Hickman, C (2009), 'The Oz Principle: Getting Results Through Individual and Organizational Accountability', Portfolio, London, UK
https://schoolsweek.co.uk/educating-drew-the-real-story-of-harrop-fold-school/
https://www.mirror.co.uk/news/real-life-stories/educating-manchester-head-drew-povey-13685899
https://www.forbes.com/sites/benjaminlaker/2020/04/02/3-ways-to-lead-through-the-coronavirus-crisis/
Mott, S (October, 2000), 'The trouble and strife of a football manager's spouse', The Telegraph, Online: https://www.telegraph.co.uk/sport/football/4774621/The-trouble-and-strife-of-a-football-managers-spouse.html, [Accessed: 21/02/2019]
Ancelotti, C. (2016), 'Quiet Leadership: Winning hearts, minds and matches', Penguin, London, UK
Snape, J, 'Managing a Mix of Characters', LMA Insights
Wooden, J (1997), 'Wooden: A Lifetime of Observations and Reflections On and Off the Court', Contemporary Books, USA
https://www.manutd.com/en/news/detail/manchester-united-announces-ole-gunnar-solskjær-as-full-time-manager
Covey, S.R. (1989), 'The 7 Habits of Highly Effective People', Simon & Schuster, London, UK
Covey, S.R. (1989), 'The 7 Habits of Highly Effective People', Simon & Schuster, London, UK
Goleman, D. (1998). Working with Emotional Intelligence. New York: Bantam Books
https://frameworkaddict.wordpress.com/2012/05/11/framework-19-golemans-emotional-intelligence-model/
Suzuki, S (2020), 'Zen Mind, Beginner's Mind: Informal talks on Zen meditation and practice', Shambala Publications, Inc., Colorado, USA
Hattie, J (2011), 'Visible Learning for Teachers: Maximizing Impact on Learning' Routledge, UK